S0-BOB-220

Jubilee 2000
CHRISTIAN ROME

The Jubilee Basilicas

THE CHURCHES, THE CATACOMBS, THE MONUMENTS

BONECHI

The inauguration of the facade of Saint Peter's Basilica restored for the Great Jubilee of the Year 2000.

© Copyright by Casa Editrice Bonechi - Firenze - Italia
E-mail: bonechi@bonechi.it - Internet: www.bonechi.it

Publication created and designed by: Casa Editrice Bonechi
Editorial management: Monica Bonechi
Graphic design and layout: Serena de Leonardis
Graphics: Laura Settesoldi
Make-up: Bernardo Dionisio
Cover: Manuela Ranfagni
Picture research: Stefano Masi, Giovannella Masini
Editing: Giovannella Masini
City and monument illustrations: Stefano Benini

Text: Stefano Masi
Translation: Paula Boomsliter

Collective work. All rights reserved. No part of this publication may be reproduced, or transmitted in any form or by any means, whether electronic, chemical, or mechanical, photocopying, or otherwise (including cinema, television, and any information storage and retrieval system) without the express written permission of the publisher
The cover and layout of this publication are the work of Casa Editrice Bonechi *graphic artists and as such are protected by international copyright and in Italy under Art. 102 of Law No.633 concerning authors' rights.*

Printed in Italy by
Centro Stampa Editoriale Bonechi - Sesto Fiorentino - Firenze

PHOTOGRAPHY ACKNOWLEDGMENTS
The majority of the photographs are property of the Casa Editrice Bonechi Archives. They were taken by Marco Banti, Gaetano Barone, Marco Bonechi, Emanuela Crimini, Gianni Dagli Orti, Serena de Leonardis, Paolo Giambone, Nicola Grifoni, Stefano Masi, MSA, Andrea Pistolesi, Gustavo Tomsich, Cesare Tonini, Michele Tonini, *and* Arnaldo Vescovo.

Other photographs were provided by:
Foto Archivio Fabbrica di San Pietro in Vaticano: *pages 24, 25, 27, 28 top, 29, 30, 31 left.*
Gaetano Barone: *page 41.*
Gianni Degli Orti: *page 79 center and top left, and page 93 bottom.*
Foto Musei Vaticani: *pages 34, 35 bottom;*
pages 35 top, 36-37, 38 bottom, 39, 40 (A. Bracchetti, P. Zigrossi); *page 38 top* (P. Zigrossi).
Foto Redazione de *L'Osservatore Romano*: *page 17 bottom right, page 18 top and bottom left.*
Photographic Service of *L'Osservatore Romano*: *pages 2-11;*
page 18 bottom right; page 42 (Arturo Mari).
Foto Pont. Comm. Arch. Sacra: *page 68, the three photos at the center and bottom.*
Scala - Istituto Fotografico Editoriale: *page 15 bottom, page 83 top.*

The publisher apologizes for any unintentional omissions. We would be pleased to include any appropriate acknowledgments of which we are informed in subsequent editions of this publication.

ISBN 88-476-0429-X

* * *

The solemn inauguration of the Holy Year

On the night of December 24, 1999, the last Christmas Eve of Christianity's second millennium, in an unparalleled setting and an atmosphere charged as never before with emotion, an estimated audience of over one billion people - the thousands upon thousands of pilgrims crowding Saint Peter's Basilica and Square and the millions who followed live television coverage in at least 58 countries throughout the world - watched the solemn ceremony of the opening of the Holy Door that officially marked the beginning of the Great Jubilee of the Year 2000. The Holy Father, wearing a magnificent gold, red and blue cape over his white vestments, was assisted by cardinals and high prelates as he performed the rite that opened this Holy Year, an event of extraordinary importance for the entire Christian world and the first in history to coincide with the end of millennium.

Thus in a moment, before the eyes of all of humanity, a new era began. Following an extremely simple yet infinitely meaningful 500-year-old ceremonial, Pope John Paul II murmured in Latin "Aperite mihi portas iustitiae" (Open for me the doors of justice) before he pushed open the door that is the concrete symbol of the Jubilee, an almost tangible threshold separating the sacred and the profane, and then knelt in prayer on the stone floor.

"Look with kindness, O Lord, on us, who in this night that is resplendent with light solemnly open the holy door and happily start the year of the Great Jubilee," the Pope said in prayers during the ceremony. "May it be a year that pleases you, a year of grace and true freedom, of reconciliation and peace." Traditionally, the Holy Door of Saint Peter's, like those of all the Jubilee Basilicas, is the last on the right on the facade of the church. Except during Holy Years, it is kept tightly closed, having been bricked up on the last day of the preceding Holy Year in remembrance of the ancient and severe rule that for centuries has dictated that the doors of the Church be closed to sinners.

This year, the solemn Christmas Eve ceremony in Saint Peter's was preceded by a number of significant preparatory events. On December 15, the brickwork of the Holy Door of the Vatican basilica was removed, in the presence of high Church officials and an anxious crowd of onlookers, and on that occasion the precious coffer that is walled up in the door during the closing ceremony of every Jubilee Year was also retrieved. The coffer contains an inestimable treasure in solid gold bricks and the keys to the Holy Door: its recovery is thus the first, ineluctable step toward the ceremonial opening of the door.

The official ceremony inaugurating the Great Jubilee

of the Year 2000, in the resplendent atmosphere that envelops Saint Peter's on Christmas Eve, incorporated a number of innovations that, however small, contrasted with the hieratic immutability of a sacred tradition that has been handed down unaltered from Jubilee to Jubilee over the centuries and underlined the relevance of Catholicism in today's multicultural world. Another significant break with tradition was that for the first time the pope did not observe the ritual of using the medieval silver hammer to break down the masonry nor even to symbolize the act that begins the opening ceremony. Although John Paul II himself had knocked three times with the hammer on occasion of the extraordinary Jubilee proclaimed in 1983, this year the frail but strong-willed 79-year-old pope simply pushed the doors wide with his hands. This was possible thanks to the fact that the brickwork had been entirely and not just loosened or partially removed as it had been since on Christmas Eve 1974 fragments detached by the hammer went flying dangerously close to the head of Pope Paul VI.

In crossing the threshold of the Holy Door, Pope John Paul II symbolically led the Church and the faithful into the heart of the Jubilee year and into the third millennium of the Christian era. The task of repeating the solemn door-opening ceremony in Rome's other Jubilee Basilicas - Saint John Lateran, Saint Mary Major, and Saint-Paul-without-the-Walls - normally goes to the cardinals specially deputed for the purpose (although this year, in another break with tradition, the Pope himself opened the Holy Door of Saint John Lateran on Christmas Day). But it is always in Saint Peter's that the first official act of the Holy Year, which symbolically infuses the heart of Christianity with a new vital force, is performed by the pope himself - and thus John Paul II conducted the Vatican Christmas Eve Great Jubilee ceremonies, which although in the main reflecting long-established custom were suffused with a special aura of participation thanks to their conjunction with such an important historical event as the dawn of the third Christian millennium.

The solemn Christmas Midnight Mass, followed by the ritual Apostolic Blessing, was an important prelude to the plenary indulgence that will be guaranteed to all those pilgrims who participate in the Jubilee Year rites in Rome. Despite the fact that it is no longer necessary to go to the Eternal City - as had been the case for centuries, on the basis of the prescriptions issued in 1300 by Boniface VIII whose tacit intent it was to increase the flow of pilgrims to the city - in order to receive the benefits of the indulgence, since this year Catholics can participate in the Holy Year celebrations and do penance on the path to indulgence even in the local dioceses, Rome continues to be the real fulcrum of the Great Jubilee of the Year 2000. It is the place where millions of followers of the Christian faith will come to celebrate not only the special ecclesiastical occasion and the start of the third millennium of Christian history, but also to discover the new face of a city that was the center of a world and the foundation of the Catholic Church - and that still continues to shine as a jewel of inestimable value in the history of all mankind.

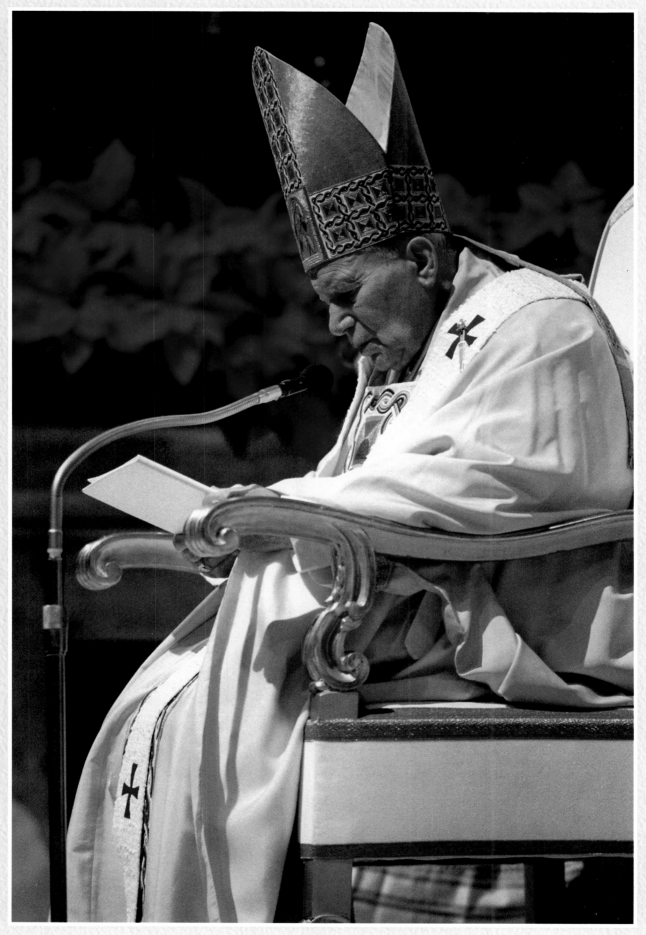

GREAT EVENTS OF THE

DECEMBER 1999

24 FRIDAY
Solemnity of the Birth of the Lord
St. Peter's Basilica
Opening of the Holy Door
Midnight Mass

25 SATURDAY
Solemnity of the Birth of the Lord
Basilica of San Giovanni in Laterano
Opening of the Holy Door
Daytime Mass
Basilica of Santa Maria Maggiore
Opening of the Holy Door
Daytime Mass

St. Peter's Basilica
"Urbi et Orbi" Blessing

Holy Land
Opening of the Jubilee
Local Churches
Opening of the Jubilee

31 FRIDAY
St. Peter's Basilica
Prayer Vigil for the Passage into the Year 2000

JANUARY 2000

1 SATURDAY
Solemnity of Mary, Mother of God
St. Peter's Basilica
Holy Mass
World Day for Peace

2 SUNDAY
Second Sunday after Christmas
St. Peter's Basilica
Day for Children

6 THURSDAY
Solemnity of the Epiphany of the Lord
St. Peter's Basilica
Holy Mass
Episcopal Ordinations

9 SUNDAY
Feast of the Baptism of the Lord
Holy Mass
Celebration of the Sacrament of Baptism for Children

18 TUESDAY
Beginning of the Week of Prayer for Christian Unity
Basilica of San Paolo fuori le Mura
Opening of the Holy Door
Ecumenical celebration

25 TUESDAY
Feast of the Conversion of Saint Paul
Basilica of San Paolo fuori le Mura
Ecumenical celebration concluding the Week of Prayer for Christian Unity

28 FRIDAY
Memorial of Saint Ephraim
Church of Santa Cecilia in Trastevere
Divine Liturgy in the Syro-Oriental Rite (Chaldean and Malabarese)

FEBRUARY 2000

2 WEDNESDAY
Feast of the Presentation of the Lord

St. Peter's Basilica
Liturgy of Light and Holy Mass
Jubilee of Consecrated Life

9 WEDNESDAY
Memorial of Saint Maron
Basilica of Santa Maria Maggiore
Divine Liturgy in the Syro-Antiochean Rite (Maronite)

11 FRIDAY
Memorial of the Blessed Virgin Mary of Lourdes
St. Peter's Basilica
Celebration of the Sacrament of the Anointing of the Sick
Jubilee of the Sick and of Health Care Workers

18 FRIDAY
Memorial of Blessed John (Beato Angelico)
Church of Santa Maria sopra Minerva
Jubilee of Artists

20 SUNDAY
Jubilee of Permanent Deacons

22 TUESDAY
Solemnity of the Chair of Saint Peter Apostle
St. Peter's Basilica
Holy Mass
Jubilee of the Roman Curia

25 FRIDAY - 27 SUNDAY
Study Convention on Implementation of the Second Vatican Ecumenical Council

MARCH 2000

5 SUNDAY
9th Sunday in Ordinary Time
St. Peter's Basilica
Beatification/Canonization

8 WEDNESDAY
Ash Wednesday
Penitential procession from the
Church of Santa Sabina to the Circus Maximus
Holy Mass and imposition of ashes
Request for Pardon

9 THURSDAY
Basilica of San Paolo fuori le Mura
Eucharistic Adoration

10 FRIDAY
Basilica of San Giovanni in Laterano
Way of the Cross and penitential celebration

11 SATURDAY
Basilica of Santa Maria Maggiore
Recital of the Rosary

12 SUNDAY
1st Sunday of Lent
Basilica of San Giovanni in Laterano
Rite of Election and the inscription of the names of the catechumens

16 THURSDAY
Basilica of San Paolo fuori le Mura
Eucharistic Adoration

17 FRIDAY
Basilica of San Giovanni in Laterano
Way of the Cross and penitential celebration

18 SATURDAY
Basilica of Santa Maria Maggiore
Recital of the Rosary

19 SUNDAY
2nd Sunday of Lent
Basilica of San Giovanni in Laterano
First scrutiny of the catechumens

20 MONDAY
Solemnity of Saint Joseph, Husband of the Blessed Virgin Mary
Jubilee of Craftsmen

23 THURSDAY
Basilica of San Paolo fuori le Mura
Eucharistic Adoration

24 FRIDAY
Basilica of San Giovanni in Laterano
Way of the Cross and penitential celebration

25 SATURDAY
Solemnity of the Annunciation of the Lord
Nazareth,
Basilica of the Annunciation
Liturgical celebration to underscore the dignity of women in the light of Mary's mission (Mulieris dignitatem), linked with the Basilica of Santa Maria Maggiore and the major Marian Shrines of the world.

26 SUNDAY
3rd Sunday of Lent
Basilica of San Giovanni in Laterano
Second scrutiny of the catechumens

30 THURSDAY
Basilica of San Paolo fuori le Mura
Eucharistic Adoration

31 FRIDAY
Basilica of San Giovanni in Laterano
Way of the Cross and penitential celebration

APRIL 2000

1 SATURDAY
Basilica of Santa Maria Maggiore
Recital of the Rosary

2 SUNDAY
4th Sunday of Lent
Basilica of San Giovanni in Laterano
Third scrutiny for the catechumens

6 THURSDAY
Basilica of San Paolo fuori le Mura
Eucharistic Adoration

7 FRIDAY
Basilica of San Giovanni in Laterano
Way of the Cross and penitential celebration

8 SATURDAY
Basilica of Santa Maria Maggiore
Recital of the Rosary

JUBILEE YEAR 2000

9 SUNDAY
5th Sunday of Lent
Basilica of San Giovanni in Laterano
Rite of giving the Creed and the
Lord's Prayer to the catechumens

13 THURSDAY
Basilica of San Paolo fuori le Mura
Eucharistic Adoration

14 FRIDAY
Basilica of San Giovanni in Laterano
Way of the Cross and penitential
celebration

15 SATURDAY
Basilica of Santa Maria Maggiore
Recital of the Rosary

HOLY WEEK

16 SUNDAY
Palm Sunday of the Passion of Our Lord
St. Peter's Square
Commemoration of the Lord's entry into
Jerusalem and Holy Mass

18 TUESDAY
Tuesday of Holy Week
Basilicas Major
Communal celebration of the
Sacrament of Penance
with individual absolution

20 THURSDAY
Holy Thursday
St. Peter's Basilica
Chrism Mass
Basilica of San Giovanni in Laterano
Mass of the Lord's Supper

21 FRIDAY
Good Friday
St. Peter's Basilica
Celebration of the Lord's Passion

Colosseum
Solemn Way of the Cross

23 SUNDAY
Easter Sunday
The Resurrection of the Lord
St. Peter's Basilica
Easter Vigil on Holy Night: Service of
Light,
Liturgy of the Word, Baptismal Liturgy
**(Celebration of the Rite
of Christian Initiation of Adults).**
Eucharistic Liturgy

St. Peter's Basilica
Daytime Mass
"Urbi et Orbi" Blessing

30 SUNDAY
2nd Sunday of Easter
Church of San Pancrazio
Mass for newly-baptized adults

MAY 2000

1 MONDAY
Memorial of Saint Joseph the Worker
Holy Mass
Jubilee of Workers (and Labor Unions)

6 SATURDAY
Basilica of Santa Maria Maggiore
Recital of the Rosary

7 SUNDAY
3rd Sunday of Easter
Colosseum
Ecumenical service for the "new martyrs"

13 SATURDAY
Basilica of Santa Maria Maggiore
Recital of the Rosary

14 SUNDAY
4th Sunday of Easter
St. Peter's Basilica
Holy Mass
Priestly Ordinations
World Day of Prayer for Vocations

18 THURSDAY
80th Birthday of the Holy Father
St. Peter's Square
Holy Mass
Jubilee of Clergy

20 SATURDAY
Basilica of Santa Maria Maggiore
Recital of the Rosary

25 THURSDAY
Jubilee of Scientists

26 FRIDAY
Church of Santa Maria degli Angeli
**Divine Liturgy in the Alexandrine-Ethiopian
Rite**
(Feast of Mary, Pact of Mercy)

27 SATURDAY
Basilica of Santa Maria Maggiore
Recital of the Rosary
28 SUNDAY
6th Sunday of Easter
Holy Mass
Jubilee of the Diocese of Rome

31 WEDNESDAY
Vigil of the Solemnity of the Ascension
of the Lord
St. Peter's Basilica
First Vespers of the Solemnity

JUNE 2000

1 THURSDAY
Solemnity of the Ascension of the Lord
St. Peter's Basilica
Holy Mass

2 FRIDAY
Jubilee of Migrants, Refugees, and Exiles

4 SUNDAY
7th Sunday of Easter
Holy Mass
Day of Social Communications
Jubilee of Journalists

10 SATURDAY
Vigil of the Solemnity of Pentecost
St. Peter's Square
Solemn Vigil of Pentecost

11 SUNDAY
Solemnity of Pentecost

St. Peter's Basilica
**Day of Prayer for collaboration among
the different religions**

18 SUNDAY
Solemnity of the Holy Trinity
Basilica of San Giovanni in Laterano
**Celebration of the opening of the
International Eucharistic Congress**

22 THURSDAY
Solemnity of the Body and Blood of Christ
Basilica of San Giovanni in Laterano
Eucharistic procession

25 SUNDAY
**Closing of the International Eucharistic
Congress**

29 THURSDAY
Solemnity of the Apostles Peter and Paul
St. Peter's Basilica
Holy Mass and the imposition of the
Pallium on Metropolitan Archbishops

JULY 2000

2 SUNDAY
13th Sunday in Ordinary Time
Station Mass of the Jubilee

9 SUNDAY
14th Sunday in Ordinary Time
Jubilee celebration in the prisons

16 SUNDAY
15th Sunday in Ordinary Time
Station Mass of the Jubilee

23 SUNDAY
16th Sunday in Ordinary Time
Station Mass of the Jubilee

30 SUNDAY
17th Sunday in Ordinary Time
Station Mass of the Jubilee

AUGUST 2000

5 SATURDAY
Vigil of the Feast of the Transfiguration of
the Lord
Basilica of Santa Maria Maggiore
Prayer vigil

6 SUNDAY
Feast of the Transfiguration of the Lord
Basilica of San Paolo fuori le Mura
Second Vespers of the Feast

14 MONDAY
Vigil of the Solemnity of the Assumption
of
the Blessed Virgin Mary
Basilica of Santa Maria Maggiore
Incense Rite of the Coptic Liturgy

15 TUESDAY
Solemnity of the Assumption of the
Blessed Virgin Mary
Opening of the 15th World Youth Day

19 SATURDAY - 20 SUNDAY
20th Sunday in Ordinary Time

Prayer Vigil and Holy Mass
Conclusion of the 15th World Youth Day
Jubilee of Youth

27 SUNDAY
21st Sunday in Ordinary Time
Station Mass of the Jubilee

SEPTEMBER 2000

3 SUNDAY
22nd Sunday in Ordinary Time
St. Peter's Basilica
Beatification/Canonization

8 FRIDAY
Feast of the Birth of the Blessed Virgin Mary
Solemn Celebration to recall the birth
of the Mother of the Lord in relation to
the
Nativity of our Saviour Jesus Christ.

10 SUNDAY
23rd Sunday in Ordinary Time
St. Peter's Basilica
Holy Mass
Jubilee of University Teachers

14 THURSDAY
Feast of the Exaltation of the Holy Cross
From the *Basilica of Santa Croce di
Gerusalemme* to the *Basilica of
San Giovanni in Laterano*
Stational Procession

Basilica of San Giovanni in Laterano
**Vespers in the Armenian Rite and
the Rite of Antasdan**

15 FRIDAY
**Opening of the International
Marian-Mariological Congress**

17 SUNDAY
24th Sunday in Ordinary Time
Jubilee of Senior Citizens

24 SUNDAY
25th Sunday in Ordinary Time
Holy Mass
**Conclusion of the International
Marian-Mariological Congress**

OCTOBER 2000

1 SUNDAY
26th Sunday in Ordinary Time
Feast of the Pokrov (Protection of the
Mother of God)

Church of Santa Maria sopra Minerva
**Divine Liturgy and the Akathistos Hymn in
the
Byzantine Rite**

3 TUESDAY
Day of Jewish-Christian Dialogue

7 SATURDAY
Memorial of Our Lady of the Rosary
Recitation of the Rosary and torchlight
procession

8 SUNDAY
27th Sunday in Ordinary Time
St. Peter's Basilica
Holy Mass
Jubilee of Bishops on occasion of the
**10th Ordinary General Assembly of the
Synod of Bishops. Act of dedicating the
new millennium to the**

protection of Mary

14 SATURDAY - 15 SUNDAY
**Third Worldwide Meeting of the Holy
Father with Families**

15 SUNDAY
28th Sunday in Ordinary Time
St. Peter's Square
Holy Mass
**Celebration of the Sacrament of
Matrimony**
Jubilee of Families

20 FRIDAY - 22 SUNDAY
**International Missionary-Missiological
Congress**

21 SATURDAY
Basilica of Santa Maria Maggiore
Celebration of the Rosary

22 SUNDAY
29th Sunday in Ordinary Time
St. Peter's Basilica
Holy Mass
World Mission Day

28 SATURDAY
Basilica of Santa Maria Maggiore
Recital of the Rosary

29 SUNDAY
30th Sunday in Ordinary Time
Olympic Stadium
Holy Mass
Jubilee of Athletes

31 TUESDAY
Vigil of the Solemnity of All Saints
St. Peter's Basilica
First Vespers of the Solemnity

NOVEMBER 2000

1 WEDNESDAY
Solemnity of All Saints
St. Peter's Basilica
Beatification/Canonization

2 THURSDAY
Commemoration of All the Faithful
Departed

4 SATURDAY
Celebration in the Ambrosian Rite

5 SUNDAY
31st Sunday in Ordinary Time
Holy Mass
Jubilee of Those Involved in Public Life

12 SUNDAY
32nd Sunday in Ordinary Time
St. Peter's Basilica
Holy Mass
Day of Thanks for the Gifts of Creation
Jubilee of the Agricultural World

19 SUNDAY
33rd Sunday in Ordinary Time
St. Peter's Basilica
Holy Mass
Jubilee of the Military and the Police

21 TUESDAY
Feast of the Presentation of the Blessed
Virgin Mary
Church of Santa Maria in Trastevere
Divine Liturgy in the Syro-Antiochene Rite
(Syrian and Malankarese)

24 FRIDAY
Opening of the World Congress for

the Apostolate of the Laity

26 SUNDAY
Solemnity of Christ the King
St. Peter's Basilica
Holy Mass
**Conclusion of the World Congress
for the Apostolate of the Laity**

DECEMBER 2000

2 SATURDAY
Vigil of the 1st Sunday of Advent
St. Peter's Basilica
First Vespers of Sunday

3 SUNDAY
1st Sunday of Advent
Basilica of San Paolo fuori le Mura
Holy Mass
Jubilee of the Disabled

8 FRIDAY
Solemnity of the Immaculate Conception
of the Blessed Virgin Mary
Basilica of Santa Maria Maggiore
Akathistos Hymn

10 SUNDAY
2nd Sunday of Advent
Basilica of San Giovanni in Laterano
Holy Mass

16 SATURDAY
Basilica of Santa Maria Maggiore
Celebration in the Mozarabic Rite

17 SUNDAY
3rd Sunday of Advent
Basilica of San Paolo fuori le Mura
Holy Mass
Jubilee of the Entertainment World

24 SUNDAY
Solemnity of the Birth of Our Lord
St. Peter's Basilica
Midnight Mass

25 MONDAY
Solemnity of the Birth of Our Lord
St. Peter's Basilica
Daytime Mass
"Urbi et Orbi" Blessing

31 SUNDAY
St. Peter's Basilica
**Prayer Vigil for the Passage into the New
Millennium**

JANUARY 2001

1 MONDAY
Solemnity of Mary Mother of God
St. Peter's Basilica
Holy Mass
World Day of Peace

5 FRIDAY
Vigil of the Solemnity of the Epiphany of
the Lord
*Basilica of San Giovanni in Laterano,
Basilica of Santa Maria Maggiore, Basilica
of San Paolo fuori le Mura*
Holy Mass
Closing of the Holy Door

Holy Land
Closing of the Jubilee

Local Churches
Closing of the Jubilee

6 SATURDAY
Solemnity of the Epiphany of the Lord
St. Peter's Basilica
Closing of the Holy Door

THE JUBILEE YEARS IN CHRISTIAN HISTORY

*T*he Christian Jubilee celebrations originate in Hebrew religious tradition. Biblical law ordered that every half-century there be declared a period of one-year's duration during which debts were remitted, slaves were freed, alienated goods were returned to their former owners, and the arable lands were redistributed. The origin of the word 'jubilee' lies in the Hebrew jobel = ram's horn, and also the name of the instrument that was sounded during the ceremony that proclaimed the Jubilee Year. The first Jubilee in Christian history was declared in 1300 by Pope Boniface VIII, who granted a plenary indulgence; that is, the remission of the temporal penalties for sin for all those faithful who, in respect of the Sacraments, having confessed their sins and received Communion, would also make pilgrimages to Saint Peter's Basilica and to the Basilica of San Paolo fuori le Mura, to the tombs of the two martyrs, at least once a day for a specified time - in the case of the inhabitants for thirty days, in the case of strangers for fifteen.

Over the centuries, the interval between one Jubilee Year and the next changed from fifty years to twenty-five; changes also came about in the modalities of celebration, the rites, and the ceremonials opening and closing the Jubilee Year, also called **Holy Year** or **Holy Year of Jubilee**. If, in fact, the bull published by Boniface VIII prescribed only visits to the tombs of the apostles Peter and Paul and to the two basilicas dedicated to them, Pope Urban VI added Santa Maria Maggiore to the list in 1390 and Martin V, in 1425, added San Giovanni in Laterano. In 1552, Saint Philip Neri lengthened to seven the list of the compulsory church visits for gaining the Roman Jubilee, by adding to the four patriarchal or greater basilicas three lesser basilicas: San Lorenzo fuori le Mura, Santa Croce di Gerusalemme, and San Sebastiano. The obligation to visit all seven of the designated basilicas remained in force until 1950, when their number returned to four. Traditionally, the Holy Year begins on Christmas Eve, when the pope opens the Holy Door, and ends a year later with its closing. Analogous ceremonies then take place in the other three patriarchal basilicas, each of which has its Holy Door. Over the course of the seven hundred years during which this tradition has been observed, there have also been proclaimed extraordinary Jubilees to celebrate especially important occasions, while other, ordinary, Jubilees were suspended for political or historical reasons of various kinds. Certain Jubilees provided the occasion for grandiose **urban renewal** projects that contributed to giving Rome the sublime monumental aspect for which it is known throughout the world. The truly important Jubilee Years declared by the Catholic Church are twenty-seven in number, if we include that of the year 2000.

Group with the figure of a pilgrim, from the frescoes by Andrea di Bonaiuto inspired by the collection of sermons by Jacopo Passavanti entitled Specchio di vera penitenza *("The Mirror of True Penitence").*

Fresco of the Jubilee of Pope Boniface VIII by an anonymous Roman painter, in San Giovanni in Laterano. Boniface VIII proclaimed the first Holy Year in 1300.

I (1300) - The first Jubilee Year in Christian history was declared by Boniface VIII Caetani, with the Papal Bull of 22 January. The text of the edict is inscribed on a stone slab in the atrium of Saint Peter's Basilica. Great political and cultural figures, among whom Carlo Martello, Dante, Giotto, and Cimabue, participated in the celebrations.

II (1350) - Proclaimed by Clement VI (Pietro Roger), during the 'exile' when the popes resided in Avignon in France, this Holy Year was superintended in Rome by a papal legate. Important figures took part in the celebration of this Jubilee, including Saint Bridget, patron saint of Sweden.

III (1390) - This was the first extraordinary Jubilee, proclaimed by Urban VI Prignano in an attempt to heal the Great Western Schism. It was continued by his successor Boniface IX Tomacelli, who also declared an unofficial Jubilee in 1400 to celebrate and propitiate the beginning of the new century.

Arnolfo di Cambio's statue of Pope Boniface and, above, a portrait of the pope. The first Jubilee in Christian history attracted many illustrious pilgrims, including Dante (shown on the right in a portrait by Domenico di Michelino).

IV (1423) - The second extraordinary Jubilee was proclaimed by Martin V Colonna to celebrate the ending of the Great Western Schism. Partial reconstruction of the city, which had suffered serious damage during the period of neglect that coincided with the exile of the papacy to Avignon, began on occasion of the announcement of this Holy Year. One of the buildings so favored was the Colonna family residence near the church of the Santi Apostoli; it provided a model for other cardinals' homes during the entire Quattrocento.

V (1450) - Nicholas V Parentucelli proclaimed this Jubilee and changed the interval between Holy Years from fifty to twenty-five years. For the occasion, the pope commissioned the Florentine architect Bernardo Rossellino to draft a plan for restructuring the city and the Vatican area (renovation of Piazza San Pietro, reconstruction of the Basilica itself, and demolition of Borgo Vecchio to make room for a straight line thoroughfare toward Ponte Sant'Angelo) to accommodate the arrival *en masse* of the Jubilee Year pilgrims; the work was completed only following the end of the Jubilee.

VI (1475) - The proclamation of this Holy Year by Sixtus IV Della Rovere was preceded by an intensive urban renovation campaign, superintended by the camerlengo Cardinal William d'Estouteville, that was destined to substantially modify the look of Rome through reorganization of the road network, construction of Ponte Sisto, decoration of the basilicas, and the building or refurbishment of a great number of hospices to care for the pilgrims, among which the Hospital of Santo Spirito in Sassia.

VII (1500) - When he proclaimed this Jubilee, Alexander VI Borgia also introduced the rite of the opening of the Holy Door, which accompanied the display of one of the most precious relics of Christendom: the *Vultur Domini* or Veronica (*vera icona* or 'true icon') preserved in Saint Peter's. The massive urban reorganization efforts that accompanied this Jubilee included the opening of Via Alessandria, which linked Saint Peter's with Ponte Sant'Angelo as had been prescribed in a project styled by Nicholas V. The year 1500 was also the date of the completion Michelangelo's first Roman work: the *Pietà* in Saint Peter's Basilica.

VIII (1525) - Declared by Clement VII de' Medici, this Jubilee was ill-attended due to the wars between Francis I and Charles V that bloodied Europe and caused the Sack of Rome in 1527. The pope

Jubilee of 1450. The straight-line thoroughfare linking the Vatican with Ponte Sant'Angelo (above), the route taken by the processions to Saint Peter's, was completed for this Jubilee.

brought some of the many substantial urban renewal works promoted by his predecessors Julius II Della Rovere and Leo X de' Medici, to completion. These projects, revolutionized the urban fabric of Rome, following the renovation of Saint Peter's Basilica, with the creation of new thoroughfares (Via Giulia, Via Leonina - today's Via di Ripetta - and the Tridente) designed to channel the influx of pilgrims toward the Vatican and the major places of worship linked to the Jubilee ceremonial.

Jubilee of 1475. For this occasion, Pope Sixtus IV (center) ordered the construction of today's Ponte Sisto (above).

IX (1550) - Proclaimed by Paul III Farnese but officially opened by Julius III, this Jubilee again saw the flocking of numerous pilgrims, who were lodged thanks to Saint Philip Neri, who founded for the purpose the Confraternity of the Holy Trinity. For the occasion - only shortly after Charles V's triumphal entry into the city - a new road link was created between Porta San Sebastiano and Saint Peter's and much urban reorganization work was carried on, including consolidation of the archaeological area lying between the Baths of Caracalla and the Campidoglio. Piazza del Campidoglio was rebuilt to Michelangelo's plans.

X (1555) - Pope Julius III Ciocchi del Monte called this extraordinary Jubilee to celebrate the promise made by Queen Mary Tudor (never fulfilled) to heal the schism between the English and the Roman churches.

XI (1575) - During the Holy Year proclaimed by Gregory XIII Boncompagni, many princes and other important figures from the world of culture and the Church visited Rome. Saint Charles Borromeo and Torquato Tasso are only two of the most illustrious names. Gregory XIII, taking his example from Sixtus IV and heralding the monumental restructuring work ordered by Sixtus V, gave a strong stimulus to the development in terms of reorganization of the urban and monumental fabric of the city.

XII (1600) - The enormous inflow of pilgrims, nearly one and one-half million, prompted Clement VIII Aldobrandini to enlarge the hospice facilities and to create special organs for their coordination. This was also the year in which Giordano Bruno was burned as a heretic in Campo de' Fiori.

XIII (1625) - Proclaimed by Urban VIII Barberini, this Jubilee was marked by a number of important, large-scale urban renewal, architectural, and artistic efforts, most of which were carried out by Borromini and Bernini. The latter was commissioned to rebuild the facade of Saint Peter's Basilica, but he was above all the author of the celebrated Colonnade in Piazza San Pietro, which he completed under Alexander VII Chigi halfway through the century.

XIV (1650) - The Jubilee Year celebrations of 1650 were presided over by Innocent X Pamphili.

XV (1675) - Although the overall number of pilgrims was low due to the conflicts that raged through Europe, the Holy Year of Jubilee proclaimed by Clement X Altieri was attended by Queen Christina of Sweden. Her visit was a stimulus for new works targeting reorganization and beautification of the city. On this occasion the Colosseum was consecrated to the memory of the martyrs during the Roman persecutions.

XVI (1700) - The celebrations were proclaimed by Innocent XII Pignatelli to reinforce the peace achieved among various European nations and were continued by Innocent's successor Clement XI.

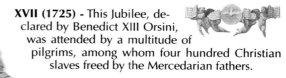

XVII (1725) - This Jubilee, declared by Benedict XIII Orsini, was attended by a multitude of pilgrims, among whom four hundred Christian slaves freed by the Mercedarian fathers.

XVIII (1750) - Like that of 1725, this Jubilee proclaimed by Benedict XIV Lambertini saw the flocking into Rome of pilgrims from all parts of the world, including the Americas and Asia.

XIX (1775) - The revolutionary storm clouds that were gathering over Europe and that exploded in France shortly afterwards induced Pio VI Braschi to cut short the duration of this Holy Year.

XX (1825) - The Jubilee of 1800 was not celebrated due to the breaking-off of relations between Napoleon's France and the Holy See; Pope Leo XII Sermattei Della Genga inaugurated the Holy Year that began 25 years later.

Jubilee of 1500. The 25-year-old Michelangelo had just completed the celebrated Pietà *in Saint Peter's Basilica (above).*

Bottom left, the statue of Giordano Bruno in Campo de' Fiori, where he was executed as a heretic in the Jubilee Year 1600.

Pope Pius XII proclaiming the end of the Holy Year 1950.

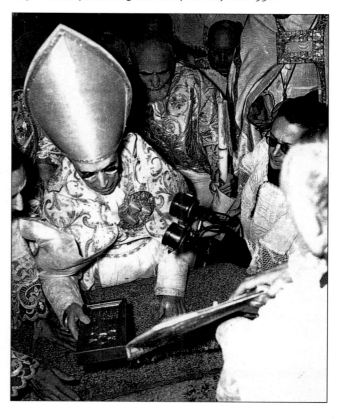

XXI (1900) - Political events in Italy - the Risorgimento movements, the wars of independence, the proclamation of the Republic of Rome, the momentary removal of the pope from Rome - forced Pius IX Mastai to suppress the Jubilees of 1850 and 1875. It was only at the beginning of the following century that Leo XIII Pecci was able to finally declare a Holy Year.

XXII (1925) - The Jubilee celebrations proclaimed by Pius XI Ratti were among the best-attended in history.

XXIII (1933) - The proclaimer of this extraordinary Jubilee, celebrating the Lateran Treaty of 1925 that regulated relations between the Holy See and the Italian state, was again Pius XI.

XXIV (1950) - The Holy Year of Jubilee proclaimed by Pius XII Pacelli strengthened international relations and brotherhood among nations following World War II.

XXV (1975) - Paul VI Montini proclaimed this Holy Year.

XXVI (1983) - The last extraordinary Jubilee of the century was declared by John Paul II (Karol Wojtyla) to celebrate the one thousand nine hundred and fiftieth anniversary of the Death of Christ. The duration of this Holy Year (394 days) was also exceptional.

XXVII (2000) - The first Jubilee of the 21st century - proclaimed by John Paul II - celebrates the two thousandth anniversary of the Birth of Christ.

Jubilee of 1975:
Pope Paul VI opening the Holy Door on Christmas Eve, 1974; pilgrims entering Saint Peter's Basilica through the Holy Door.

Pope John Paul II proclaiming the Jubilee of 1983.

THE JUBILEE BASILICAS

MAJOR

SAINT PETER'S

SAN GIOVANNI IN LATERANO

SANTA MARIA MAGGIORE

SAN PAOLO FUORI LE MURA

MINOR

SAN LORENZO FUORI LE MURA

SAN SEBASTIANO

SANTA CROCE IN GERUSALEMME

THE VATICAN

*Center of Christendom, fulcrum of Western spiritual life, and bastion of the Roman Catholic religion, for ages expression of the glory of the Church Triumphant, the Vatican rises the ancient Ager Vaticanus. In a certain sense the name, derived from vaticinio = vaticination, foreshadowed even in the pagan era the destiny of the site. Here stood Nero's Circus, actually begun under Caligula and only completed by the sadly famous emperor during whose reign Saint Peter, the first shepherd of the Church and a central figure in its history, was martyred. The **tomb of the apostle**, who was buried on the exact spot on which he died, soon became a shrine where many faithful came to pray; so much so that following the Edict of Milan (313) that acknowledged the right to practice the Christian religion, the emperor Constantine ordered construction of a grandiose basilica on the site. Work began a few years later.*

*The **Basilica di San Pietro in Vaticano (Saint Peter's Basilica)** thus arose in all its magnificence and in a very short time became a key site in Christian geography. Charlemagne was crowned Holy Roman Emperor here on Christmas Day of the year 800; this event marked the Vatican's acquisition of a precise political connotation in addition to its established spiritual power. Enclosed by the **Leonine Walls** by order of Pope Leo IV, the area, theretofore outside the city pomoerium, became an integral part of the urban fabric of Rome. Nevertheless, for another five centuries the Lateran remained the seat of the highest ecclesiastical offices and the center of papal power. Construction during the 13th century filled the space around Saint Peter's with buildings designed to house certain administrative bodies of the Roman Curia.*

*Under Nicholas III, two Dominican monks and architects named Sisto and Ristoro enlarged the original papal palace from which the complex of the **Vatican Palaces**, later adapted to contain the **Vatican Museums** collections, arose. One of their efforts was the Palatine Chapel, on which the **Sistine Chapel** was later built; another a walled garden in which the **Palazzetto del Belvedere** was later erected. With the return of the papacy to Rome in 1377 following its 'exile' to Avignon, the Vatican was chosen as the permanent residence of the popes. There thus began construction work that was to employ hosts of architects and artists for centuries.*

*Nicholas V advanced the idea of rebuilding the basilica, but work began only in 1506 under Julius II. Bramante's plans were later substituted by designs by Michelangelo, who in the same period also created the **dome of Saint Peter's** and the **Sistine Chapel frescoes**.*

*With Paul V and Maderno, the basilica took on its final form, while the decoration of the interior continued during the pontificate of Urban VIII with work conducted by Gian Lorenzo Bernini, also author of **Piazza San Pietro (Saint Peter's Square)**. From the Vatican, the popes have uninterruptedly, for centuries, exercised their spiritual and temporal powers. The pope still enjoys jurisdictional power over that which, following the Lateran Treaty of 11 February 1929, is defined as **Vatican City**, the smallest sovereign state in the world. The pope, who is elected by his cardinals during conclaves held in the Sistine Chapel (the word 'conclave' derives from the fact that these secret meetings are held with the doors closed cum clave; that is 'by key'), holds full legislative, executive and judiciary powers in the state, besides being recognized as the supreme power in the world Catholic community.*

Vatican City mints its own coins and prints its own stamps, supports a radio station, and prints a daily newspaper, L'Osservatore Romano. Order is kept by the famous Swiss Guard, the Vatican police force instituted in 1506, and the security service created in the 1800s.

Aerial view of Saint Peter's Square and Basilica.

Vatican Gardens - An almost perfectly preserved, 16th-century style Italian formal garden.

Fontana dell'Aquilone Built by Giovanni Vasanzio, the fountain takes its name from the enormous tufa stone eagle atop the rock.

Radio Vaticana - The first station was set up by Guglielmo Marconi in 1931, not far from today's studios, located in a bastion of the ancient Leonine Walls, once home to the astronomical observatory.

Palazzo del Governatorato - Built in the 1930s as the home of the Vatican City administrative offices.

Santo Stefano degli Abissini - Founded by Leo II, the church was granted to the Coptic friars in 1479 by Pope Sixtus IV.

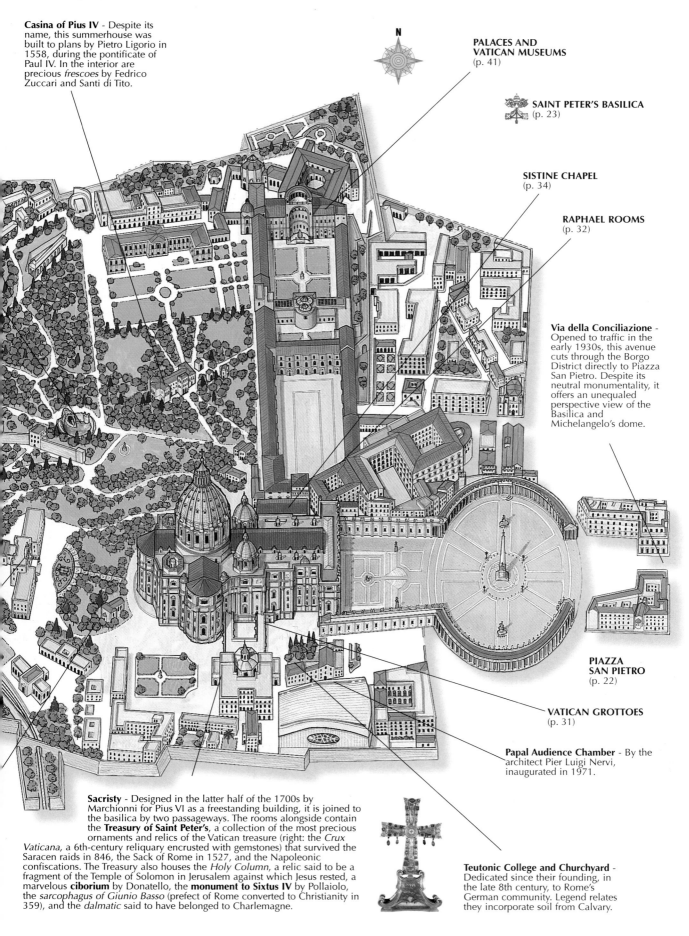

Casina of Pius IV - Despite its name, this summerhouse was built to plans by Pietro Ligorio in 1558, during the pontificate of Paul IV. In the interior are precious *frescoes* by Fedrico Zuccari and Santi di Tito.

N

PALACES AND VATICAN MUSEUMS (p. 41)

SAINT PETER'S BASILICA (p. 23)

SISTINE CHAPEL (p. 34)

RAPHAEL ROOMS (p. 32)

Via della Conciliazione - Opened to traffic in the early 1930s, this avenue cuts through the Borgo District directly to Piazza San Pietro. Despite its neutral monumentality, it offers an unequaled perspective view of the Basilica and Michelangelo's dome.

PIAZZA SAN PIETRO (p. 22)

VATICAN GROTTOES (p. 31)

Papal Audience Chamber - By the architect Pier Luigi Nervi, inaugurated in 1971.

Sacristy - Designed in the latter half of the 1700s by Marchionni for Pius VI as a freestanding building, it is joined to the basilica by two passageways. The rooms alongside contain the **Treasury of Saint Peter's**, a collection of the most precious ornaments and relics of the Vatican treasure (right: the *Crux Vaticana*, a 6th-century reliquary encrusted with gemstones) that survived the Saracen raids in 846, the Sack of Rome in 1527, and the Napoleonic confiscations. The Treasury also houses the *Holy Column*, a relic said to be a fragment of the Temple of Solomon in Jerusalem against which Jesus rested, a marvelous **ciborium** by Donatello, the **monument to Sixtus IV** by Pollaiolo, the *sarcophagus of Giunio Basso* (prefect of Rome converted to Christianity in 359), and the *dalmatic* said to have belonged to Charlemagne.

Teutonic College and Churchyard - Dedicated since their founding, in the late 8th century, to Rome's German community. Legend relates they incorporate soil from Calvary.

PIAZZA SAN PIETRO (SAINT PETER'S SQUARE)

A sacred, uniquely evocative setting, imbued with profound religious and symbolic connotations: Piazza San Pietro is perhaps the most famous square in the world. Since the Middle Ages it has welcomed and been a gathering place for countless multitudes of pilgrims come to visit Saint Peter's Basilica, the center of Christianity, and has offered a vital space for the functions of the religious life of the city. The square was built over a part of the ancient Vatican Circus (or Nero's Circus, though in reality built almost entirely during Caligula's reign), of which there remains the so-called **Vatican Obelisk**, transported here in 37 BC from Alexandria, where it decorated Caesar's Forum. Called in medieval times the *aguglia*, it stood at length beside the basilica, until in 1596 Sixtus V ordered Domenico Fontana to move it to its present site. In 1613, Paul V bid Carlo Maderno build a **fountain** to its right; half a century later, a 'twin' fountain by Carlo Fontana, placed symmetrically with respect to the first, was added. Again under Sixtus V, the original bronze globe that topped the obelisk (today in the Capitoline Museums), and that was believed to contain the ashes of Caesar, was replaced with that pope's family emblem, the mountains and the star, topped by a crucifix containing a fragment of the Holy Cross of Christ's Crucifixion.

In the mid-17th century, when the monumental work of rebuilding Saint Peter's Basilica was well-delineated, attention naturally shifted to the square before it, which was built by Gian Lorenzo Bernini between 1656 and 1667. The feeling of triumphal spectacularism lent by the genius of the Baroque architect and sculptor to this immense masterpiece was not entirely dictated by artistic considerations; he also imbued his design with profound symbolic significance, to the point that the entire opus may be interpreted as a monumental allegory.

The great **portico** that opens out from the facade of the basilica to form two hemicycles delineated by a quadruple row of Tuscan columns supporting an entablature animated by a procession of *statues of saints* and the immense *coats-of-arms* of Pope Alexander VII, during whose reign the work was realized, is a symbolic embrace by the Church that would welcome and protect all the faithful of the world in this life and in that to come. The vast elliptical space (240 meters in width), so theatrically defined by the two hemicycles, is also possessed of many symbolic references. Arisen as the last forum of Rome and dedicated to Christianity, it owes its form to that of the circuses of the ancient *Urbe*, and in particular to the Colosseum: the square may thus be said to play the role of historical *trait-d'union* between the early Church, persecuted as were its martyrs who in the amphitheaters were put to death, and the glory of the Church Triumphant, in which Christ and the saints portrayed in the statues are participants. But the elliptical form is also evocative of the Firmament, in which, according to the theory of Copernicus, coeval with construction of the square, the planets describe such orbits, and of the Universe, understood as the space-time dimension in which the obelisk, which stands at the geometrical center of the ellipse and is the gnomon of an immense sundial, symbolizes the sun and alludes to the all-importance of the pope, the Vicar of Christ on Earth.

Saint Peter's Square, Via della Conciliazione, and the Borgo district seen from above Saint Peter's Basilica.

SAINT PETER'S BASILICA

The original Saint Peter's basilica was ordered built by Constantine on the site on which0en buried, and from the very first the sanctuary drew crowds of faithful pilgrims. Begun in 324, the enormous five-aisled structure was completed only in 349, although it had already been consecrated and opened to worship in 326.

A great number of sacred buildings, oratories, cloisters, and baptisteries, were later built all around the monumental basilica, and all were decorated with precious mosaics, statues, and various, refined ornaments of different provenance. The complex reached the Renaissance intact; in 1452, Pope Nicholas V commissioned Rossellino to enlarge the apsidal portion of the basilica. But another half century was to pass before the original structure was completely revolutionized,

Saint Peter's Basilica. Michelangelo's dome and the facade.

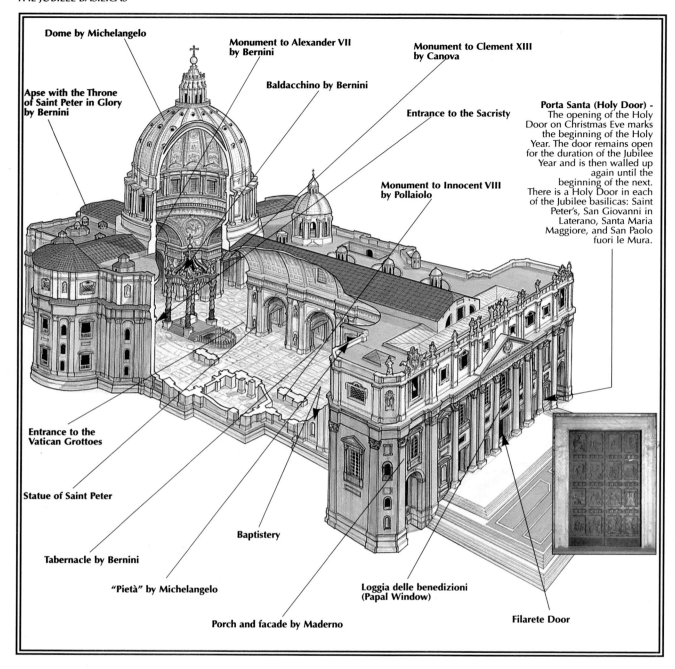

Dome by Michelangelo

Monument to Alexander VII by Bernini

Monument to Clement XIII by Canova

Apse with the Throne of Saint Peter in Glory by Bernini

Baldacchino by Bernini

Entrance to the Sacristy

Porta Santa (Holy Door) - The opening of the Holy Door on Christmas Eve marks the beginning of the Holy Year. The door remains open for the duration of the Jubilee Year and is then walled up again until the beginning of the next. There is a Holy Door in each of the Jubilee basilicas: Saint Peter's, San Giovanni in Laterano, Santa Maria Maggiore, and San Paolo fuori le Mura.

Monument to Innocent VIII by Pollaiolo

Entrance to the Vatican Grottoes

Statue of Saint Peter

Baptistery

Tabernacle by Bernini

"Pietà" by Michelangelo

Loggia delle benedizioni (Papal Window)

Filarete Door

Porch and facade by Maderno

when Pope Julius II commissioned Bramante to renovate the basilica. The architect from the Marches region of Italy demolished the earlier edifice almost in its entirety, also making a clean sweep of the structures that has risen around it in order to make room for a grandiose building that according to his plans would have been on a Greek cross plan with a central dome. At Bramante's death Raphael took over and suggested transforming the structure into a Latin cross by lengthening the entrance bay, while retaining the idea of the dome. The two designs alternated for years as supervision of works passed from one architect to another; finally, in 1546, Michelangelo again opted for Bramante's original design, while making slight modifications to the dimensions and the structure to make it smaller and slimmer, and to the design of the **dome**, which although based on Brunelleschi's cover for Florence's cathedral appeared absolutely innovative and revolutionary. Thus the dome, completed by Giacomo Della

Porta and Domenico Fontana in 1588-89, consisted of a tambour supported by 16 buttresses hidden by binate columns; between the columns of each pair open the large windows with tympana. The double-shell dome reaches upward above the tambour in sections with 16 ribs, on which three orders of oculi open.

To the sides are two **small domes**, by Vignola, with purely decorative functions and not in correspondence to the Clementine and Gregorian Chapels underneath.

At the death of the master from Tuscany, supervision of works again passed from hand to hand among many architects, until under Pope Paul V the Latin cross plan returned to favor. Maderno added three chapels per side and lengthened the nave as far as the present **facade**, which he completed in 1614. On 18 November 1626, in the one thousand three hundredth anniversary year of the original consecration, Urban VIII finally consecrated the new basilica. Maderno's work to a certain extent penalized Michelangelo's project by obstructing the full view of the dome, which is visible only in part behind the monumental facade with gracious *clock faces* by Valadier at either end. On either side of the facade stand two huge neoclassical statues of *Saint Peter* and *Saint Paul*.

The announcement of the election of a new pope is made from the central balconied window on the facade, known as the **Loggia delle benedizioni**, from which papal blessings are normally given. The **porch**, proportionally as vast as the interior, is imaginatively and elegantly decorated with statues, friezes, and stuccowork; it shelters the *Navicella mosaic*, designed by Giotto for the original basilica but restored and moved many times, showing *Christ inviting Peter to walk on the water*. Five entrances open at the back of the porch: the stupendous central **portal**, which leads in to the basilica, is a 15th-century work by Filarete; the last on the right is the **Holy Door**, which is solemnly opened by the pope to inaugurate Jubilee Years, and closed during another just as solemn ceremonial at the end of each.

The **interior**, in all its seeming boundlessness, is the symbol of the Church Triumphant, and the profuse and opulent decoration only accentuates the sublime atmosphere of the glorification of Christianity.

This feeling of monumentality emerges from a simple glance at the **nave**, with its *ceiling* that was richly decorated under Pius VI in 1780, the *stars* set into the floor to indicate the size of the world's largest churches, the *holy water stoups* supported by massive marble putti, and the venerated **statue of the seated Saint Peter** imparting the blessing, probably by Arnolfo di Cambio, near the last pillar on the right.

But as soon as he crosses the threshold, the visitor's eye is

Porch of Saint Peter's Basilica. The 'Navicella' mosaic designed by Giotto.

Saint Peter's Basilica. A view of the interior.

drawn by the great bronze **Baldacchino** with its tortile columns. It is the fruit of felicitous collaboration by Bernini, Borromini, and Duquesnoy that absorbed the artists' energies from 1624 through 1633.

Under the host of angels that crowns the daring structure, almost 30 meters in height and for the construction of which Pope Urban VIII Barberini sacrificed the Pantheon bronzes, is the *papal altar* at which only the pope may celebrate Mass; it stands over the *confessio*, decorated by Maderno and illuminated by 95 eternal flames, built over the tomb of Saint Peter. Above the Baldacchino, the inner shell of Michelangelo's dome is decorated with *mosaics* designed by the Cavalier d'Arpino.

In the space behind the altar, in the colossal **apse** or tribune, is the splendid **Throne of Saint Peter in Glory**, a late work by Bernini (1656-1665), who pressed into service all his astounding art as a sculptor and decorator in a complex play of stucco, gilt work, sculptures, and reliefs. The *bronze throne* supported by the statues of the *Doctors of the Church* contains the wooden throne that (historically unfounded) tradition relates was used by Saint Peter. To the left of the monumental tribune is the *monument to Pope Paul III* by Guglielmo Della Porta; to the right, Bernini's *monument to Pope Urban VIII*.

The first chapel in the **right aisle**, decorated by Bernini in such a manner as to mask the narrowing at the third arch, where Maderno's extension is grafted to Michelangelo's original structure, contains the celebrated **Pietà** by Michelangelo, sculpted by the Tuscan master in 1498-1499 for the Charles VIII's legate to the Holy See. The third is the *Chapel of the Holy Sacrament*, which contains Bernini's resplendent **Tabernacle**, a ciborium inspired by Bramante's Tempietto di San Pietro in Montorio and flanked by two kneeling angels.

Beyond the *monument to Gregory XIII*, the author of the reform of the calendar that now bears his name, is the *Gregorian Chapel* completed by Giacomo Della Porta in 1583.

Further on, the **right transept** gives access to the *Chapel of Saint Michael* with before it the **monument to Clement XIII**, a masterpiece by Canova dating to about 1790.

Across the apse on the left side of the

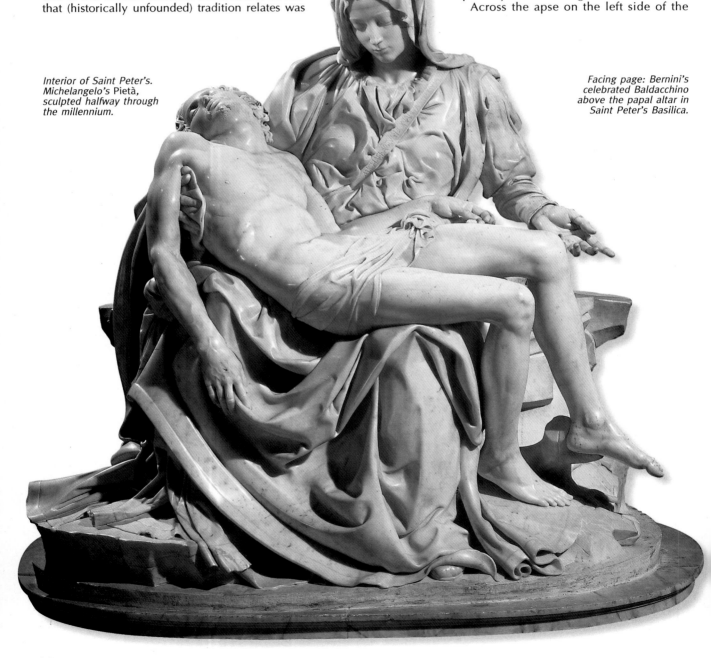

Interior of Saint Peter's. Michelangelo's Pietà, *sculpted halfway through the millennium.*

Facing page: Bernini's celebrated Baldacchino above the papal altar in Saint Peter's Basilica.

Interior of Saint Peter's.
The statue of Saint Peter attributed to Arnolfo di Cambio, and Bernini's 'Gloria', centering on the Throne of Saint Peter.

Left, a view of the interior of Michelangelo's dome.

Interior of Saint Peter's. Bernini's monument to Pope Alexander VII, created using a rich array of marbles.

basilica is the corresponding *Colonna Chapel* containing the relics of Saint Leo I the Great, to whom the beautiful marble altarpiece by Algardi showing *Leo the Great Halting Attila* alludes.

In the adjacent passageway a somber skeleton holding an hourglass calls attention to Bernini's **monument to Pope Alexander VII** that introduces the **left transept**. Past the *Clementine Chapel*, built like the corresponding chapel in the right aisle by Della Porta, is the **left aisle** with the lavish *Choir Chapel*.

In the following passageway is the bronze **monument to Innocent VIII** cast by Pollaiolo in 1498. At the level of the first chapel is another masterpiece by Canova, the *Stuart Monument*, tomb of the last members of the family; the grace of the two genies with their upside-down torches is striking. Last to open on the nave is the **baptistery**, with its *baptismal font* adapted from an ancient Roman sarcophagus.

Interior of Saint Peter's.
Left, the bronze monument to Pope Innocent VIII by Pollaiolo.

Below, Canova's monument to Clement XIII.

The tomb of Saint Peter.

Interior of Saint Peter's, Chapel of the Holy Sacrament. Bernini's Tabernacle, inspired by Bramante's Tempietto di San Pietro in Montorio.

VATICAN GROTTOES

This important sacred site underneath the Vatican basilica contains the mortal remains of the popes and the *tomb of Saint Peter*, over which the first church was raised. The intricately configured series of rooms in the Vatican Grottoes may be divided into three principal areas. The first are the **Old Grottoes** that extend through a vast cavity between the floor of the present basilica and that of the original building, under the nave and aisles of the upper construction. They contain the **tombs** of many popes, including that of *Boniface VIII* (who proclaimed the first Jubilee Year) by Arnolfo di Cambio, and those of the most recent popes like *John XXIII*, *Paul IV*, and *John Paul I*, but also the sepulchers of important temporal rulers such as *Emperor Otho II* and *Queen Christina of Sweden*. Many of the altars, sculptures, frescoes, and mosaics that decorated the original basilica are also installed here. The **New Grottoes**, called thus because their restoration postdates that of the Old Grottoes, are arranged in a semicircle with many radial chapels alternating with niches with statues of the *Apostles* by Mino da Fiesole and other masters of the same period. The whole is built around the **Chapel of Saint Peter**, built on the site of the tomb of the first pope and richly decorated under Clement VIII.

The Bocciata Chapel contains the interesting 14th-century fresco by Pietro Cavallini of the *Madonna and Child* that once adorned the atrium of the old basilica.

A third level underlying the Vatican Grottoes as such is host to a large **pre-Constantinian necropolis**, dating to the first through the fourth centuries. Among the many pagan tombs there are also those of Christians, including the original burial place of Saint Peter.

SAINTS PETER AND PAUL IN ROME

The early history of the Roman church is linked to the figures of Saints Peter and Paul as emblems of Christian doctrine. Their presence in Rome had a profound influence on the religious and historical destinies of the city both during their lifetimes and afterward. Many important religious sites recall the two saints. First among them is **Saint Peter's Basilica**, built where the apostle was martyred and buried. Peter, originally named Simon, was born in Bethesda in the 1st century BC. He was a fisherman when he was called to be a disciple of Jesus at the beginning of his ministry. He received from Jesus the name Cephas (in Aramaic, 'rock'; hence Peter, from the Latin *petra*). Jesus also gave Peter a certain precedence over the other apostles (Matthew 16:13-20) just as the popes, as the successors of Peter, have primacy over the bishops. After the death of Christ and the descent of the Holy Spirit on the apostles, Peter preached at length in Jerusalem, where he was arrested in about 41 AD. He escaped from prison with the help of an angel, who broke his chains, the same that later miraculously united with the chains that held the apostle in Rome and that are still venerated in the Roman church of **San Pietro in Vincoli**.

From Palestine, Peter took refuge in Rome, where for almost 20 years he found hospitality in many homes, including that of the patrician Pudens, where the church of **Santa Pudentiana** stands today. According to tradition, Peter was again captured and imprisoned in the **Mamertine Prison**, where he baptized his jailers and then escaped disguised in a slave's cape, his feet bandaged because of the sores from his chains. In flight along the Appian Way, after losing his bandages where the church of **Santi Nereo ed Achilleo** now stands, he encountered Christ at the site of today's church of '**Domine quo vadis?**' and decided to return to Rome to face his martyrdom. He was martyred in 64 or 66 at Nero's Circus in the **Vatican**, crucified head down.

St. Paul was martyred in the same period on the Via Laurentina. The Apostle of the Gentiles was beheaded and, according to tradition, his head rebounded three times, giving rise to three founts, later to be marked by the **Abbazia delle Tre Fontane** (Abbey of the Three Fountains). Paul's body was moved to a cemetery on the Via Ostienses, where the **Basilica di San Paolo** was built. Born in Tarsus into a Jewish family, Paul was a soldier of the Roman army. He was converted as the result of a vision on the road to Damascus and preached throughout Greece and Asia Minor. He arrived in Rome in 61, bound in chains and awaiting Imperial judgment. Found innocent, he departed for Spain, returning to Rome three years later and living, according to tradition, in a house near the present church of **San Paolino alla Regola** where he was arrested.

RAPHAEL ROOMS

The master began frescoing what are now known as the Stanze di Raffaello (Raphael Rooms) in 1509. The work, which continued into the following years under Leo X, revolves around themes that celebrate the power of Faith and the Church.

The first room to be frescoed was the **Room of the Segnatura**, called thus because it was here that the pope signed official documents; Raphael's sure touch gleams from all the frescoes, from the *Dispute of the Blessed Sacraments*, depicting the glorification of the Eucharist, to the *School of Athens*, which brings together in a grandiose architectural frame the wise men and the philosophers of ancient times and the seigneurs and the artists of the Renaissance cultural scene, all gathered around the figures of Plato and Aristotle, and to the *Parnassus*, an allegorical celebration of the arts impersonated by the mythological figures of the Muses and the pagan gods. In the alternating medallions and panels of the ceiling, almost as a symbolic compendium of the frescoes on the walls below, Raphael painted allegorical representations of the Sciences and the Arts (*Theology, Justice, Philosophy, Poetry, Astronomy*) together with emblematic episodes referred to them (*Adam and Eve*, the *Judgment of Solomon, Apollo and Marsyas*).

From 1512 to 1514, Raphael worked on the decoration of the **Room of Heliodorus**, where he frescoed historical episodes that at once illustrate divine intervention in favor of the Church and glorify the salient episodes of Julius II's reign, according to an iconographic program dictated by the same pope. *Leo I Halting Attila* alludes to the Battle of Ravenna in 1512 at which the future Leo X defeated the French; the *Miracle at Bolsena* illustrates the institution of the Corpus Domini by Urban IV and also calls to mind the vow made by Julius II before the siege of Bologna; the biblical episode of the *Expulsion of Heliodorus from the Temple* refers to the pope's struggle against the enemies of the Church; the *Liberation of Saint Peter* alludes to the liberation of Leo X from his imprisonment after the Battle of Ravenna. The next two years, until 1517, were dedicated to the **Room of the Fire in the Borgo**, which takes its name from the principal fresco, *The Borgo Fire of 847 AD*, inspired by the figure of Leo IV who extinguished the fire by making the sign of the cross. This and the other frescoes in the room (the *Battle of Ostia*, the *Oath of Leo III*, the *Coronation of Charlemagne*), executed almost entirely by Raphael's pupils under the strict guidance of the master, make specific reference to Leo III and Leo IV, illustrious predecessors of Leo X, during whose pontificate the room was decorated. The **Sala dei Palafrenieri** also contained wall paintings by Raphael, which were destroyed and later replaced by other frescoes ordered by Gregory XIII in the late 1500s.

The decoration of the **Hall of Constantine** is instead certainly the work of one of Raphael's most important followers, Giulio Romano. Following the death of the master he led a team of artists who illustrated in fresco episodes from the life of Constantine: the *Baptism of Constantine*, the *Battle of the Milvian Bridge*, the *Apparition of the Cross*, and *Constantine's Donation*.

Room of Heliodorus. Raphael, Expulsion of Heliodorus from the Temple.

Room of the Segnatura. Raphael, School of Athens *and* Dispute of the Blessed Sacraments.

THE SISTINE CHAPEL

Between 1475 and 1481, Pope Sixtus IV charged Baccio Pontelli with design of a new pontifical chapel; the vast rectangular hall with a barrel-vaulted ceiling was built by Giovannino de' Dolci. Mino da Fiesole, Giovanni Dalmata, and Andrea Bregno subdivided the space into two parts with a marble *choir screen* and also created the *Cantoria* or choristers' gallery, while a veritable host of great artists participated in the pictorial decoration, including figures of such caliber and renown as Botticelli, Ghirlandaio, Perugino, Luca Signorelli, and Cosimo Rosselli.

In 1506, Julius II decided to have the **ceiling**, which at the time was blue and strewn with stars, frescoed as well, and entrusted the immense project to the genius of Michelangelo, already employed in reconstruction of Saint Peter's Basilica. The Tuscan master began painting the vast surface (almost 800 square meters) in May of 1508, and completed the work four years later. Michelangelo's composition consists of a series of Old Testament scenes; continuity is assured by plastic and pictorial architectural elements in which emblematic and symbolic figures provide narrative 'hinges' and iconographic links among the different episodes. Michelangelo's innovative colors have been revealed in all their original splendor by recent restoration.

The twelve figures in question are **Prophets and Sibyls**, the heralds of the coming of the Messiah: *Jeremiah*, the *Persian Sibyl*, *Ezekiel*, the *Erythraean Sibyl*, *Joel*, *Zachariah*, the *Delphic Sibyl*, *Isaiah*, the *Cumaean Sibyl*, *Daniel*, the *Libyan Sibyl*, and lastly *Jonah*, in ecstasy at the moment of his exit from the whale's belly. Together with the vigorous pairs of *Ignudi* supporting garlands and medallions, the twelve figures frame the nine panels of the **Stories of the Genesis**: *God Dividing Light from Darkness*; *God Creating the Sun and the Moon and Plants*; *God Dividing the Waters from the Land and Creating the Fishes and the Birds*; the incredibly famous **Creation of Adam** and the *Creation of Eve* at the center; *Original Sin*; the *Sacrifice of Noah*; the *Flood*; and the *Drunkenness of Noah*. In the triangles at the four corners of the vault are other biblical episodes: *Judith and Holophernes*, *David and Goliath*, the *Punishment of Haman*, and the *Brazen Serpent*. The lunettes and the spandrels over the windows contain equally splendid frescoes of the **Ancestors of Christ**. Twenty-five years after completing the ceiling, Michelangelo returned, at Pope Paul III's bidding, to crown his opus with a great fresco on the back wall of the chapel. Thus in 1536-1541 the artist created what many feel is his absolute masterpiece - the **Last Judgment**, centering on the figure of Christ Judge surrounded by a superbly innovative composition of the hosts of the elect and the damned - for the realization of which the earlier frescoes by Perugino had to be destroyed.

Sistine Chapel. One of the lunettes with a figure from the 'Ancestors of Christ' series by Michelangelo, following restoration.

Facing page, Sistine Chapel. Michelangelo's frescoes of the Creation of Adam *(above) and* Original Sin *(below) on the ceiling, following restoration.*

On the following pages:

In the foldout, an overall view of the ceiling of the Sistine Chapel frescoed by Michelangelo, following restoration.

Sistine Chapel. 15th century frescoes on the side walls. Above, Scenes from the Life of Moses by Sandro Botticelli; below, Moses' Journey into Egypt by Perugino.

Sistine Chapel. Overall view of the Last Judgment *by Michelangelo, following restoration.*

Sistine Chapel. View of a side wall, with above, frescoes by Michelangelo: figures of the 'Ancestors of Christ' in the lunettes, and below, four figures from the series of 'Popes'. In the lower band, 15th-century frescoes by Perugino, Handing Over the Keys to Saint Peter, and Cosimo Rosselli, Last Supper.

Above, a bird's-eye view of the Vatican Museums.

VATICAN MUSEUMS

From the very first, the complex that is today called the **Palazzi Vaticani** has hosted splendid collections of art assembled by the various popes. The supreme pontiffs also enriched their collections by patronizing the arts and employed entire generations of Italian and foreign artists in the creation of masterpieces on commission.

The many collections, from those of Greek, Roman, Etruscan, and Egyptian antiquities to those of books and paintings (the latter now in the celebrated **Pinacoteca Vaticana**) slowly filled the available rooms, halls and galleries as they were built - and in many cases provided the impetus for their construction.

The arrangement of the collections has changed over the centuries in relation both to the increase in available space and to changes in the criteria in vogue for the organization and cataloging of works in museums, and the buildings gradually became museums to all effects. The first step in this direction was taken in the late 1700s by Clement XIV, who transformed the Palazzetto del Belvedere into the museum that, following the reorganization ordered by Clement's successor Pius VI, took the name of **Museo Pio-Clementino**.

In the first half of the following century, that passion for archaeology and antiquity that was a hallmark of Neoclassical taste induced two popes, Pius VII and Gregory XVI, to create certain of the cardinal institutions of the Vatican museum complex: the former founded the **Museo Chiaramonti**, to the decoration of which even Canova contributed and for which the Braccio Nuovo was expressly built; the latter pope organized the **Museo Gregoriano Etrusco** and the **Museo Gregoriano Egizio** in seventeen rooms.

Later on in the 19th century, Pope Leo XIII opened to the public many rooms which theretofore had been reserved for the pope and the highest members of the ecclesiastical hierarchy. The first such revelation was the Borgia Apartments, which later became the seat of the **Collection of Modern Religious Art** inaugurated by Pope Paul VI in 1973. The creation of new museums went on all through the twentieth century: John XXIII had both the **Museo Missionario Etnologico**, instituted in 1926 to house the material exhibited at the Missionary Exhibit of the 1925 Jubilee, and the **Museo Pio-Cristiano**, founded in 1854 by Pius IX to organize the paintings, inscriptions, reliefs and sculptures from the catacombs and the ancient Roman basilicas, moved to the Vatican from their original homes in the San Giovanni in Laterano complex.

Pope John Paul II at the window of the Papal Apartments and pilgrims in Saint Peter's Square; right, an aerial view of Saint Peter's Basilica and Square.

BASILICA DI SANTA MARIA MAGGIORE

Tradition has it that on the night of August 5, 356, during the pontificate of Saint Liberius, the Virgin appeared to both the pope and a noble Roman, showing them the Esquiline, the ancient *Mons Cispius*, covered with snow and asking them to build a sanctuary in her name at its summit. When snow was found on the hill the following morning, the pope ordered that there be built around the whitened perimeter a basilica, which he called Liberiana after himself, and Santa Maria ad Nives, after the miraculous event. In reality, the date does not correspond historically to that of the basilica of Santa Maria Maggiore, which was instead consecrated by Pope Sixtus III following the Council of Ephesus in 431. Despite the many restorations carried out over the centuries, the plan of the building is still for the most part that of an early Christian basilica; as a whole, the building is a living text of the history of art and architecture, incorporating as it does chapters from the Romanesque through the late Baroque.

In the **facade** alone this intermingling of vastly different elements can be appreciated in all its magnificence: the 18th-century **portico** by Ferdinando Fuga precedes the medieval facade, featuring splendid 13th-century polychrome **mosaics** representing the *Miracle of Saint Mary of the Snow*. The contrast is repeated in the juxtaposition of the two 17th-century structures that link the facade to the tall **campanile**, still Romanesque although dating from the 14th century. The **apsidal facade,** also from the 1600s, is a work of great harmony by Carlo Rainaldi, who managed to connect with an elegant yet simple structure the two symmetrical 16th-century **cupolas** that cover the Sistine and Pauline chapels.

The interior of the basilica is strikingly original in appearance. The essential lines of the original 5th-century structure contrast with the later coffered ceiling by Giuliano da San Gallo, who decorated it with the first gold brought from the Americas. The 36 mosaic panels of *Scenes from the Old Testament* that adorn the walls of the **nave** date to the 5th century, although they feature some significant later alterations. The mosaics in the **apse** provide a superb corollary to those of the nave: the mosaic of the triumphal arch represents *Events in the Life of Jesus* and dates to the founding of the church, while those of the apsidal vault depict the *Coronation of the Virgin* and

Santa Pudenziana - The church was built over the house of the Roman senator Pudens, whose daughters were the Saints Praxedes and Pudentiana; Pudens was known to have provided hospitality to St. Peter during his apostolate in Rome. The ancient *titulus*, perhaps dating from the 2nd century, was replaced in the late 4th century by a church, which, although extensively rebuilt during the Middle Ages and the Renaissance, is still partially visible in the present building. Works carried out during medieval times are evident on the exterior with the Romanesque **campanile**, from the early 13th century, and the facade, with its lovely **portico** featuring two antique fluted columns and an 11th-century frieze representing the *Lamb of God* with *Saints Peter, Pudens, Pudentiana and Praxedes*. Inside, the apse contains splendid *mosaics* from the 4th century with *Christ Triumphant* enthroned and surrounded by the *Apostles* and the *Saints Pudentiana and Praxedes*, who are offering crowns. In the background are the *Cross, Heavenly Jerusalem*, and the *symbols of the Evangelists*. Also of note is the **Caetani Chapel**, on the left side of the nave, begun by Francesco da Volterra in 1598 and completed by Maderno in 1614.

San Lorenzo in Panisperna - The church, which rises above a double stairway next to a shaded courtyard with several **medieval houses**, was built under Constantine on the site of the saint's martyrdom. It was restored in the early 1300s and again in the 1500s, when the **campanile** was added. The interior contains frescoes, attributed to Pasquale Cati and influenced by the work of Michelangelo, that depict the *Martyrdom of Saint Laurence*.

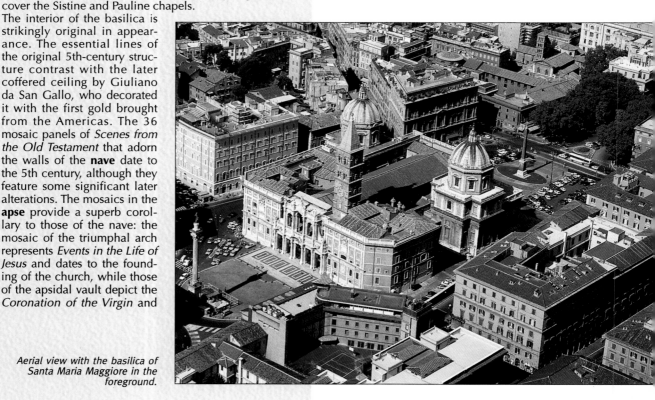

Aerial view with the basilica of Santa Maria Maggiore in the foreground.

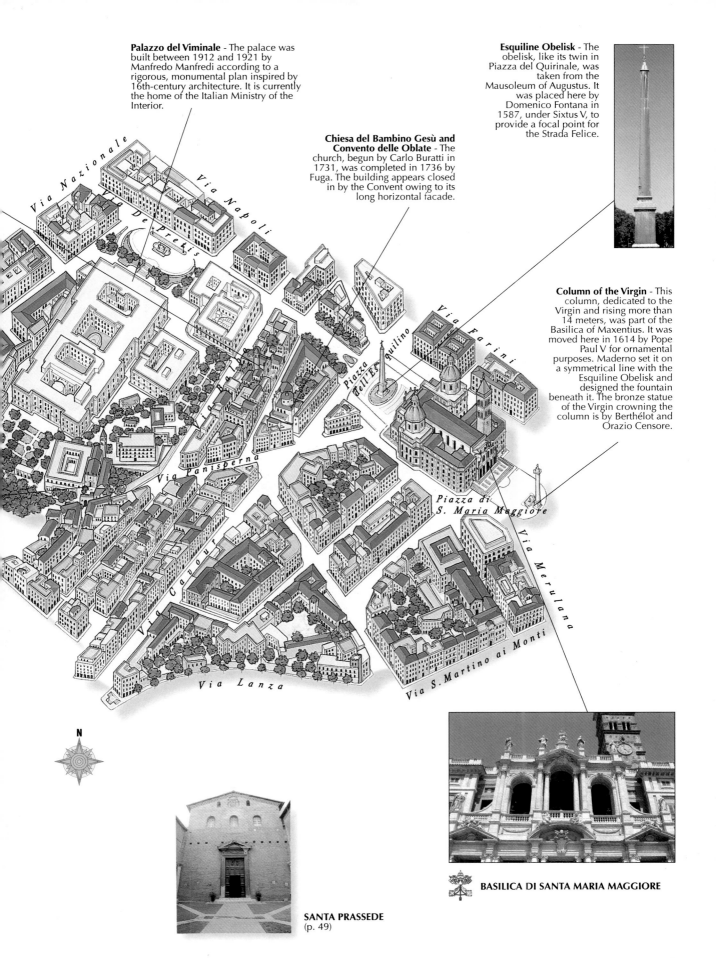

Palazzo del Viminale - The palace was built between 1912 and 1921 by Manfredo Manfredi according to a rigorous, monumental plan inspired by 16th-century architecture. It is currently the home of the Italian Ministry of the Interior.

Chiesa del Bambino Gesù and Convento delle Oblate - The church, begun by Carlo Buratti in 1731, was completed in 1736 by Fuga. The building appears closed in by the Convent owing to its long horizontal facade.

Esquiline Obelisk - The obelisk, like its twin in Piazza del Quirinale, was taken from the Mausoleum of Augustus. It was placed here by Domenico Fontana in 1587, under Sixtus V, to provide a focal point for the Strada Felice.

Column of the Virgin - This column, dedicated to the Virgin and rising more than 14 meters, was part of the Basilica of Maxentius. It was moved here in 1614 by Pope Paul V for ornamental purposes. Maderno set it on a symmetrical line with the Esquiline Obelisk and designed the fountain beneath it. The bronze statue of the Virgin crowning the column is by Berthélot and Orazio Censore.

Via Nazionale

Via Napoli

Via De Pretis

Via Panisperna

Via Cavour

Via Lanza

Piazza dell'Esquilino

Via Farini

Piazza di S. Maria Maggiore

Via Merulana

Via S. Martino ai Monti

N

SANTA PRASSEDE
(p. 49)

BASILICA DI SANTA MARIA MAGGIORE

Santa Maria Maggiore, with its 18th-century facade, the richly decorated interior of the Pauline Chapel, and the frescoed cupola by Cigoli.

were produced in 1295 by Jacopo Torriti, who also made the mosaics that originally adorned the apse of San Giovanni in Laterano. Also interesting are the *baldacchino* by Fuga and the **confessio**, restored in the 1800s by Vespignani to hold the relics of the crib of the Infant Jesus. The great profusion of art works produced in different periods that decorate the aisles and their chapels are perhaps too overwhelming to be seen in just one visit. At the beginning of the **right aisle** is the *Baptistery*, built by Flaminio Ponzio in 1605 and adorned with frescoes by Passignano and beautiful sculptures.

Opening at the end of the aisle is the **Sistine Chapel**, commissioned from Domenico Fontana by Sixtus V in 1585 for his *funerary monument*, which is placed next to the tomb of Pius V. The chapel, built in the full spirit of the Counter Reformation and decorated with marble from the *Septizodium* on the Palatine, is topped by a cupola and has two smaller side chapels. In the chapel is the entrance to the **Oratory of the Holy Nativity**, which originally housed the relic of the Crib of the Infant Jesus and is still home to a fine crêche. The statues of *Saint Joseph*, the *Magi*, the *oxen*, and the *ass* are by Arnolfo da Cambio; those of the Virgin and the Infant Jesus by Valsoldo.

A curiosity: Gian Lorenzo Bernini is buried here in the family tomb, marked by a simple stone.

In perfect symmetry with Sistine Chapel is the **Pauline**

Chapel at the end of the **left aisle**. Commissioned by Pope Paul V to house his *sepulchral monument*, the chapel was completed by Flaminio Ponzio in 1611 following the same plan of its twin chapel on the right side. However, this chapel contains works of even greater artistic value: the painted decorations are by some of the most important artists of the Baroque age. The frescoes on the cupola are by Cigoli, while those on the spandrel are by the Cavalier d'Arpino. The paintings on the lower sections of the chapel are instead by Guido Reni and Passignano. The genius Rainaldi designed the **altar**, with its beautiful decorations in semi-precious stone, while a bas-relief by Maderno, inspired by the mosaic on the medieval facade, depicts *Pope Liberius tracing the perimeter of the basilica*. The altar contains a fine Byzantine *Madonna*, which according to tradition was painted by Saint Luke.

Santa Maria Maggiore. The cupola of the Sistine Chapel.

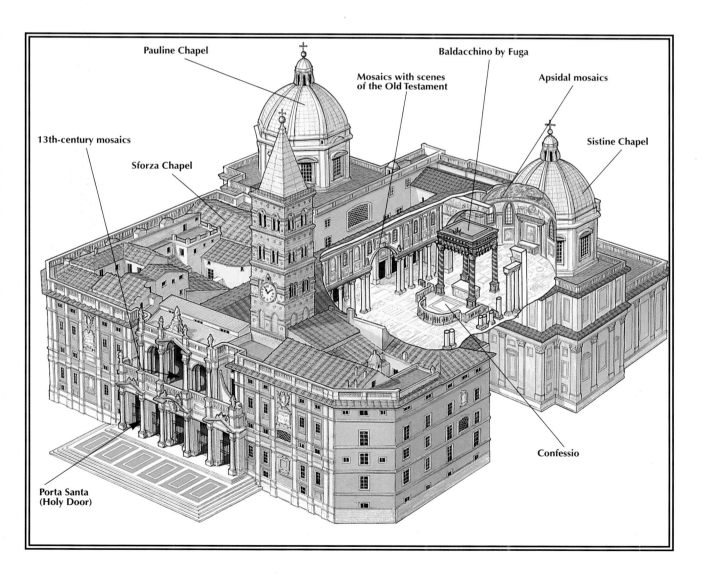

Pauline Chapel

Baldacchino by Fuga

Mosaics with scenes of the Old Testament

Apsidal mosaics

13th-century mosaics

Sforza Chapel

Sistine Chapel

Porta Santa (Holy Door)

Confessio

The last among the numerous master-pieces of this church is the **Sforza Chapel**, designed by Michelangelo in 1564, the year of his death, and executed by his pupil Giacomo Della Porta.

On the left, views of Santa Maria Maggiore. From top to bottom, the mosaics on the facade, a view of the wooden ceiling by Giuliano da Sangallo, and a detail of the apsidal mosaic by Jacopo Torriti of the Coronation of the Virgin (late 13th century).

Above right, Santa Prassede, Chapel of San Zeno. Detail of the vault.

Below, right, the splendid apsidal mosaics of Santa Pudenziana with Triumphant Christ surrounded by the figures of the Apostles and of Saints Pudentiana and Praxedes offering crowns (4th century).

SANTA PRASSEDE

This early Christian basilica, still almost intact in its essential design and containing some of the most beautiful masterpieces of high medieval mosaics, was built in the 5th century on the site where Saint Praxedes and her sister Pudentiana, daughter of the Roman senator Pudens, gathered the remains of some 2,000 martyrs of the Christian church in a well before they themselves were martyred for their gesture of piety and religious faith. Around the well stood the ancient *titulus*, upon which Pope Paschal I had the basilica built in the 9th century. The church has undergone only partial alterations, including the addition of several pilasters that support the 13th-century wooden ceiling. The brick **facade** also dates from the 9th century, and the 15th-century doorway is preceded by a court and a double atrium with an external Romanesque **portico**.

In the **interior**, medieval pilasters and 16 columns, which support an architrave partially composed of antique fragments, separate the aisles from the central nave, while a porphyry disk on the pavement near the entrance marks the spot where the well of Saint Praxedes was located. Fine **mosaics** dating from the time of Paschal I adorn the apse and the Chapel of Saint Zeno. The **triumphal arch** in front of the presbyterian enclosure is decorated with a mosaic of *Celestial Jerusalem*, approached by the crowds of the Elect: at the top is the image of *Christ among the Angels and Saints*, including Saint Praxedes and her sister Saint Pudentiana. The area of the **presbytery,** with a ciborium in the center, is decorated with the *Twenty-four Elders of the Apocalypse*, who extend their arms offering crowns to the *Lamb of God*, the *Archangels*, the *Evangelists,* and the *Apostles*, here symbolically represented. The **apsidal bowl** instead presents the *Redeemer* among *Saints Peter, Paul, Praxedes, Pudentiana, Zeno* and *Paschal I*, who is shown presenting a model of the church and with a square halo because he was still living when the mosaics were produced. Below is a strip showing the *Lamb of God* with 12 other *sheep*, symbolizing the Apostles, the two *holy rivers* and the two *holy cities*, Jerusalem and Bethlehem.

The **Chapel of San Zeno**, once called the 'Garden of Paradise', opens towards the aisle with a front composed of a Classical doorway flanked by two columns, an inset window with an antique urn placed in front of it, and a mosaic with *Christ*, the *Virgin* and *Saints*. But the masterpiece of this chapel created by Paschal I in honor of his mother Theodora, who is buried here and portrayed with a square halo in the niche on the left side, is without doubt the **vault**, in which four *Angels* hold a medallion with an image of *Christ*. Around this, other figures form part of the retinue of the *Madonna*, perhaps a later work, depicted in the niche of the altar. In the adjacent small chapel is the so-called *Column of the Flagellation*, a venerated relic brought here from Jerusalem in the Middle Ages and said to be the one at which Jesus also was scourged. The church also contains other works of great value and beauty: the *funerary monument of Bishop Santoni* is the first work executed by Bernini in Rome (1614); the interesting the **confessio** houses two *sarcophagi* containing the bodies of the two sister saints and numerous other *relics* of martyrs.

Santa Prassede. The interior and a detail of the triumphal arch and apse.

The Chapel of San Zeno in Santa Prassede. The mosaics on the vault and above of the entrance.

Porta Asinara - Originally, this was a minor gateway from which issued the Via Asinara; it was enlarged by order of Honorius, who also added the enclosure around the entrance and the two semi-cylindrical towers.

BASILICA DI SAN GIOVANNI IN LATERANO

Porta San Giovanni - Built by Jacopo Del Duca during the pontificate of Gregory XIII, in 1574, to replace the older Porta Asinara.

Triclinium of Leo III - Repaired in the 18th century and enclosed in a sort of exedra by Ferdinando Fuga, the mosaic portraying *Christ and the Apostles, Saint Peter Crowning Leo III, and Christ Investing Pope Sylvester and Constantine* is all that remains of the dining room (*triclinium*) of the ancient Patriarchate, the papal palace commissioned by Leo III in the late 8th century.

Scala Sancta - The 16th-century building was commissioned by Sixtus V. As we read in an inscription in the interior, it unites in a single building the **Scala Sancta** itself and the **Chapel of Saint Lawrence** or *Sancta Sanctorum* (Holy of Holies). According to a 15th-century tradition, the staircase is that of Pilate's praetorian palace, up which Jesus walked to submit to Roman judgment. Tradition again dictates that it be climbed by the faithful on their knees, reciting specific prayers on each of the 28 steps. The *Sancta Sanctorum* is instead a surviving portion of the original papal palace built in the late 1200s during the pontificate of Nicholas III. It is decorated with fine Cosmati work and contains extremely precious relics, including the celebrated image of the *Savior* called the *Acheiropoeton*; that is, not painted by human hand but the product of prodigious divine intervention.

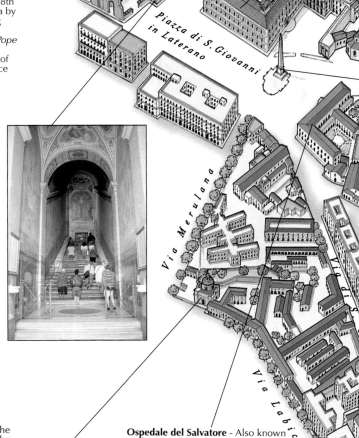

Lateran Obelisk - This most ancient and tallest of Rome's obelisks was transported here in 1587 by Domenico Fontana from the Circus Maximus, where it had been raised by order of Constantius II in 357. It was originally part of the Egyptian Temple of Ammon in Thebes.

Santi Marcellino e Pietro - The ancient church dedicated to the two martyrs and saints was founded in the 4th century; it was totally rebuilt in 1751 by Girolamo Theodoli in forms that show the influence of Borromini both in the interior and in the stepped dome.

Ospedale del Salvatore - Also known as the **Ospedale di San Giovanni**, this hospital was founded in 1348 by the Compagnia del Santissimo Salvatore *ad Sancta Sanctorum*, and remodeled during the 15th century. The facade on the square is the 17th-century work of Carlo Rainaldi and Giacomo Mola.

Piazza di Porta S. Giovanni

Piazza di S. Giovanni in Laterano

Via Merulana

Via Labicana

Via di S. Giovanni in Laterano

Viale S. Quattro Coronati

50

Lateran Palace - Domenico Fontana built today's palace for Sixtus V in 1586-1589 on the earlier Patriarchate, for centuries the papal residence, of which it retained the original layout. The massive, squared-off building, with its distinctive three almost identical facades, takes its inspiration from the models typical of the sober Counter-Reformist style in architecture, of which Palazzo Farnese is the outstanding example. Beginning in the mid-19th century, the Lateran Palace became the home of the Museo Gregoriano Profano, the Museo Pio-Cristiano, and finally, in the 1920s, the Museo Missionario Etnologico; all three collections are now in the Vatican. Today, the Lateran is home to only the **Museo Storico Vaticano**: it occupies the rooms of the papal apartments, which include the Sala della Conciliazione built on the ancient Hall of the Popes of the Patriarchate.

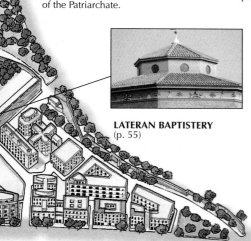

LATERAN BAPTISTERY
(p. 55)

THE COSMATI MASTERS

Between the 12th and 13th centuries, a succession of several generations of marble workers, decorators, and architects working in Rome created some of the most interesting works of the late Romanesque period. These works were characterized by precious polychrome marble inlays and by mosaic highlights achieved by applying glass paste or gold tesserae to structures (cloisters, campanile, pavements) or to religious objects (ambones, thrones, altars, ciboria).
The denomination 'Cosmati' comes from *Cosma*, a particularly common name among the members of the various family groups that for two centuries perpetuated this artistic tradition. The first 'Cosmati worker' was Paolo, the founder of the family, who with his sons made the ciborium for **San Lorenzo fuori le Mura** in or around 1148.
The most important family unit was the one headed by Lorenzo, who with his son Jacopo and grandson Cosma worked on restoration of several churches during the 12th century (**Santa Maria in Trastevere, San Clemente, Santa Maria in Cosmedin**). The Cosmati of the Vassalletto family continued the tradition in the 13th century; among their many works are the cloisters of **San Giovanni in Laterano** and **San Paolo fuori le Mura**.

SANTI QUATTRO CORONATI
(p. 56)

BASILICA DI SAN GIOVANNI IN LATERANO

The cathedral of Rome and the ancient center of papal power during the entire Middle Ages, the Basilica of San Giovanni in Laterano was founded by Pope Melchiades in 311-314 on land belonging to the Plauzi-Laterani family granted to him by the wife of the emperor Constantine. It is therefore also the oldest Christian basilica in the world, since its foundation predates that of Saint Peter's by about fourteen years. San Giovanni also differs from Saint Peter's in the very different way in which it was constructed, having been restructured and rebuilt a little at a time with no single project and above all proceeding with the idea of preserving the primitive structure. And indeed, although it underwent sometimes quite radical renovation, the layout of the basilica is still quite similar to the original.
Thus, if on the one hand the **foundations** incorporate the remains of the very oldest structures, the exterior walls are those of the early Middle Ages, although reinforced, while the cloister and the two **bell towers** date to the 13th century.
The work conducted in the 1500s by Domenico Fontana and by Giacomo Della Porta included the **transept** and the **side facade** erected near the papal window commissioned by Sixtus V. The first of these creations was frescoed by a group of Mannerist painters, under the direction of the Cavalier d'Arpino, with *stories from the Bible*, *scenes from the life of Constantine*, and salient phases of the *construction of the basilica*.
We might say that until the 16th century the internal structure of the building, with a nave and four aisles divided by tall stands of columns and enhanced by a fine Cosmatesque **floor**, remained almost intact. But its condition was so critical that on occasion of the Jubilee of 1650 Innocent X had the **interior** completely remodeled by Borromini and although the artist was constrained in his work by considerations of conservation, he nevertheless succeeded admirably in expressing his genius as an architect. In the **nave**, he left intact the beautiful wooden **ceiling**, designed by Piero Ligorio and decorated by Daniele da Volterra in 1562-1567, and limited his intervention to creating in the twelve pillars the same number of recesses to receive *statues of the Apostles*.
In the four **aisles**, he preferred simple decoration with heads of angels and cherubs, and instead highlighted the architectural purity of the pillars, arches, and vaults. Here, Borromini excogitated a genial decorative solution that reused the many sculptures of the *medieval and Renaissance tombs*, in Baroque aediculae of his own design. One of these, at the first pillar of the intermediate right aisle, instead houses a fragment of a fresco, attributed to Giotto, of *Pope Boniface VIII announcing the first Holy Year in 1300*. Not far from this aedicula are others with the funeral monuments of prelates, nobles, and famous popes: *Sylvester II*, who in the Middle Ages was known as a worker of miracles, *Alexander III*, and *Sergius IV*.
Another interesting monument is that in the intermediate left aisle to *Elena Savelli*, decorated by Jacopo Del Duca, a qualified pupil of Michelangelo's, with an expressive bust and refined reliefs, all in bronze.

The Lateran Obelisk, of ancient Egyptian origin.

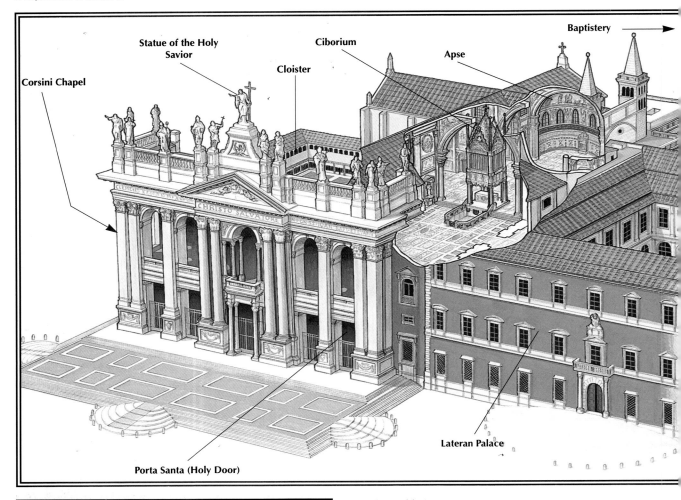

Baptistery

Statue of the Holy
Savior

Ciborium

Apse

Cloister

Corsini Chapel

Lateran Palace

Porta Santa (Holy Door)

San Giovanni in Laterano.
The 13th-century cloister, a masterpiece of
Cosmati marblework.

San Giovanni in Laterano.
The main facade, a view of the interior showing
the Cosmatesque-style floor, and a view of
the wooden ceiling.

The **confessio**, instead, contains the funeral monument to *Pope Martin V*; the tombstone is a masterpiece of the Renaissance by the Florentine artist Simone Ghini.

Above, almost as though it were watching over the **papal altar**, at which only the pope is permitted to celebrate Mass, is the Gothic-style **ciborium** made for Urban V in 1367 by Sienese masters and ornamented with twelve panels frescoed by Barna da Siena; it contains, in silver *reliquaries*, the heads of the apostles Peter and Paul.

The **apse**, beyond the presbytery, was completely remodeled under Leo XIII, who commissioned reinstatement of the original mosaic by Jacopo Torriti (also the author of that in Santa Maria Maggiore) and Fra' Jacopo da Camerino, whose self-portraits are the two figures kneeling alongside the *Apostles* between the windows.

Off the far left aisle open two of the basilica's masterpieces, the Corsini Chapel and the **cloister**, in which in the third

decade of the 13th century the Cosmati of the Vassalletto family demonstrated their skillful hand with marble. The cloister is a vast arched portico with small columns of differing forms, some of which are highlighted with mosaic.

Above the archways runs a richly-adorned entablature, also decorated with mosaics and sculpted marble lions' heads; under the portico are some remains of the architecture and decoration of the ancient basilica, among which fine sculptures taken from the *funeral monument to Cardinal Annibaldi* by Arnolfo di Cambio, and the original bronze door of the Scala Sancta. The **Corsini Chapel** is instead the work of the Tuscan architect Alessandro Galilei, who built it in 1732-1735 to contain the funeral monument to Pope Clement XII Corsini with the *statue* of the pope by Giovan Battista Maini. Galilei was also the author of the solemn, monumental main **facade**, on which stands the *statue of the Holy Savior* surrounded by those of the titular saints of the basilica, *John the Baptist* and *John the Evangelist*, and those of the *Doctors of the Church*.

Interior of San Giovanni in Laterano. A view of the presbytery.

In the interior of San Giovanni in Laterano, the frescoed panels of the ciborium.

LATERAN BAPTISTERY

This small and very ancient building, also known as San Giovanni in Fonte, is essentially that commissioned by Constantine. It was nevertheless amply remodeled many times, most importantly in the 5th century under Sixtus III and in 1657 under Urban VIII.

The octagonal plan, the model for many a later baptistery, reveals an interior organized around a central space delimited by two orders of overlapping porphyry and white marble columns, at the center of which stands a green basalt *urn* with a bronze cover, once used for baptism by immersion.

All around are chapels: the **Chapel of Saint John the Baptist** preserves the massive 5th-century bronze *doors*; the **Chapel of Saint Venantius** and the **Chapel of Saint Rufina** are still decorated with fine *mosaics* from the 5th and 7th centuries, respectively; the **Chapel of Saint John the Evangelist** also boasts a bronze *portal* dating to 1196 and *mosaics* from the second half of the 5th century.

Top, one of the 12 statues of the apostles that line the nave of San Giovanni in Laterano.

Lateran Baptistery. The interior, with the circle of two superposed orders of columns; below, the mosaics of the narthex.

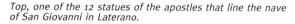

SANTI QUATTRO CORONATI

This church, erected in the 4th century, was dedicated to the four soldiers Severus, Severianus, Carpophorus, and Victorinus, who according to an ancient tradition were martyred because they refused to kill four Dalmatian sculptors who had in turn refused to sculpt the likeness of a pagan divinity. Other sources name the sculptors as the martyrs, but whatever turn events actually took, the church has always been the chosen place of worship of Rome's stone-cutters and marble-workers.

The original building was renovated in the 9th century and later, after having been destroyed by the Normans, was rebuilt under Pope Paschal II. The convent, the cloister, and the Oratorio di San Silvestro were added in the 12th and 13th centuries.

The entrance, under an arch surmounted by a distinctive Romanesque **bell tower**, opens on a series of **courtyards** and **porticoes** that lead to the church proper. The three-aisled **interior**, with its *women's gallery*, is one of the most extraordinary surviving examples of medieval architecture, and is all but perfectly intact. The columns supporting the asymmetrical archways, the Cosmatesque *floor* in part composed of ancient Roman paving stones, and the remains of many frescoes all suggest to the church's evocative past.

The enormous **apse**, which embraces all three aisles, was decorated in the 17th century by Giovanni da San Giovanni with frescoes of the *Martyrdom of the Four Crowned Saints* and the *Glory of All Saints*, which includes some angels with curious female traits that earned for the work the nickname of '*Coro delle Angiolesse'*.

Santi Quattro Coronati.
A view of the cloister and two of the frescoes in the Oratorio di San Silvestro depicting Scenes from the History of Saint Sylvester and Constantine*; on the top left,* Emperor Constantine kneeling as he donates the symbolic tiara to Saint Sylvester (the 'Donation of Constantine').

Under the presbytery is the **crypt**, where the relics of the four titular martyrs are preserved. The left aisle instead gives access to the **cloister** of the convent, with its distinctive archways supported by small columns adorned with water lily leaves; at the center is a singular *fount* for ablutions, from the time of Paschal II.

The second exterior courtyard of the church leads into the **Oratorio di San Silvestro**, with its perfectly-preserved original decoration painted in 1246 by Venetian masters of Byzantine training, showing the *Last Judgment* and *Scenes from the History of Saint Sylvester and Constantine*. An ancient legend recounts how the emperor's leprosy was healed by the saint, who Constantine had called in after Saint Peter and Saint Paul had appeared to him in a dream; Sylvester cured the emperor by baptism and in gratitude the emperor granted him lands by a document known in history as the Donation of Constantine. But the historical inaccuracy of the story was proven in the 15th century by Lorenzo Valla.

Nero's Aqueduct - This aqueduct was built by Nero as a branch of the *Aqua Claudia* to supply the *Domus Aurea* on the Oppian hill and the nymphaeum of the Temple of the Divus Claudius on the Caelian hill. Domitian extended it to the Palatine to supply water to the imperial residence.

BASILICA DI SAN LORENZO FUORI LE MURA (p. 59)

Piazza di Porta Maggiore

Via Statilia

Via S. Croce in Gerusalemme

Via Eleniana

Piazza S. Croce in Gerusalemme

Porta Maggiore - Originally built by the emperor Claudius in 38 AD to allow the *Aqua Claudia* and *Anio Novus* aqueducts to bridge the *Via Praenestina* and the *Via Labicana*, this structure was later incorporated into the Aurelian Walls. The architectural composition, with two openings with aediculae and columns formed of blocks of travertine, is striking.

Tomb of Eurysaces - This sepulcher of the late republican era, apparently that of the rich baker Marcus Vergilius Eurysaces, came to light in 1838 following the demolition of the bastions erected by Honorius. The structure, which much influenced the architecture of the Fascist era, includes a relief showing Eurysace overseeing bread-making.

Castrense Amphitheater - This construction, begun by Septimius Severus and completed by Elagabalus, was originally part of the Sessorian Palace, the private home of the last emperors of Rome. It was later incorporated in the Aurelian Walls, from which its first-story arches and columns emerge.

N

BASILICA DI SANTA CROCE DI GERUSALEMME

Santa Croce di Gerusalemme. Cross by Valadier (1803).

BASILICA DI SANTA CROCE DI GERUSALEMME

Perhaps the most important of the three minor Jubilee basilicas, Santa Croce di Gerusalemme has been known since the Middle Ages as the 'basilica of the relics' due to the great number of mementos of saints and martyrs it contains. Its official name derives from the soil of the Holy Sepulcher in Jerusalem brought here by Constantine's mother Saint Helena and placed, together with the precious relics of the Cross and the Passion of Christ, in a hall of her private home, the Sessorian Palace. The atrium was converted some decades later into a church, called the Sessorian Basilica after the palace; it was completely rebuilt in the 12th century by Pope Lucius II.

The **bell tower**, with its Cosmatesque aediculae, and the **cloisters** are the only external elements to have survived the 18th-century restoration promoted by Pope Benedict XIV and performed by Domenico Gregorini and Pietro Passalacqua, authors of the creative convex **facade** inspired by Borromini's style. The two architects also transformed the medieval narthex into a luminous and lively elliptical **atrium** that nevertheless preserves traces of the original decoration in the fine

The atrium and a detail of the facade of Santa Croce di Gerusalemme; below, the interior with the 18th-century baldachin and the fresco in the apse.

14th-century crucifix frescoed in the adjoining left chapel.

The **interior** is divided into a nave and two aisles by twelve columns, four of which are enclosed in the 18th-century pillars. Although architecturally less successful, it is by no means less significant, with its beautiful wooden *ceiling*, the false vault of which is decorated with the *Apotheosis of Saint Helena* by Giaquinto, who was also the author of the paintings decorating the **apse** and the **presbytery** - to the exception of the *Legend of the Holy Cross*, a masterful 15th-century fresco by Antoniazzo Romano. Over the 16th-century *tomb of Cardinal Quiñones*, by Sansovino, in the back of the apse, stands the marble and gilded bronze *tabernacle* designed by Maderno. To the right of the apse, steps lead to the **Chapel of Saint Helena**, founded by Constantine, that contains the soil of the Holy Sepulcher under its floor; the titular saint is portrayed in a modified Roman statue on the altar. The **mosaic** that adorns the upper portion of the walls and the vault is a Renaissance work variously attributed to Melozzo da Forlì and Baldassare Peruzzi.

The adjacent Gregorian Chapel was commissioned by Cardinal Carvajal, whose tomb is in the apse. Of less artistic and architectural importance, but of inestimable religious value, is the **Chapel of the Relics**, containing the fragments of the True Cross, the Holy Thorns of Christ's Crown, a portion of the cross of Saint Dismas the Good Thief, and other significant sacred relics. The **Sessorian Library**, in the adjoining convent, is also of interest with its frescoes by Pannini.

BASILICA DI SAN LORENZO FUORI LE MURA

Although severely damaged by the World War II bombings, San Lorenzo still preserves much evidence of its remote and illustrious past. In truth, it arose from the fusion of the Pelagian Basilica, dedicated to Saint Lawrence, and Honorius' church dedicated to the Virgin, commissioned by the popes Pelagius II (6th century) and Honorius III (13th century), respectively. The Pelagian Basilica stood alongside the primitive Constantinian building that was destined for purely cemeterial functions and contained the relics of the titular saint, which were later moved to the adjacent Pelagian building. The lovely **portico** created by the Vassalletto family Cosmati workers, incorporating ancient columns with Ionic capitals, dates to the 13th century; under the portico are a number of *ancient tombs* and remains of medieval *frescoes*. Alongside are the monastery, with its beautiful **cloister**, and the late 12th-century Romanesque **bell tower**.

The **interior** shows evident signs of the origin of the building as the fusion of two churches that while contiguous were laid out on different axes: the front portion has a nave and two aisles divided by twenty-two ancient columns; the rear church, which forms the presbytery and the apse of the present-day basilica, has three aisles divided by columns that probably came from the earlier Constantinian building and upper **women's galleries**, marked out by small columns with a Byzantine cast. Examples of the alacritous activity of the Cosmati can also be found in the interior of the basilica: the beautiful mosaic *floor*, unfortunately damaged by the WWII bombings, the two *pulpits*, the *ciborium*, the *paschal candelabrum* and the *bishop's throne* at the back of the choir.

The **mosaic** that decorates the triumphal arch with *Jesus with Saints Paul, Stephen, Hippolytus, Peter, Laurence and Pope Pelagius* instead dates to the 6th century.

San Lorenzo fuori le Mura. The Romanesque bell tower and the 13th-century portico; below, the bishop's throne with the Cosmati work frontals, and a view of the cloister.

Rocca dei Savelli and **Giardino degli Aranci** - Of the fortress built under Alberic II in the 10th century and taken by the Savelli near the turn of the first millennium, only the ramparts remain. The area, with its cluster pines and orange trees, was owned by the Dominicans of the adjacent Santa Sabina before being made a public park in the 1930s.

Monument to Mazzini - The statue of the hero of the Risorgimento, or Italian unification, was made by Ettore Ferrari in 1929 and placed here for the centenary of the Roman Republic.

Santi Bonifacio e Alessio - The original Romanesque building dates to the 8th century, but the primitive plan was greatly distorted when the church was redesigned several times in the 16th and 18th centuries. The intact *crypt* contains the relics of Saint Thomas of Canterbury. In the 18th-century interior behind the doorway erected by Honorius III are parts of the Cosmatesque floor and two small Cosmatesque columns in the apse. The well in the left aisle reputedly belonged to the house of Saint Alexis, as did the staircase, in a precious Baroque frame, under which the saint slept. The bell tower is from the 13th century.

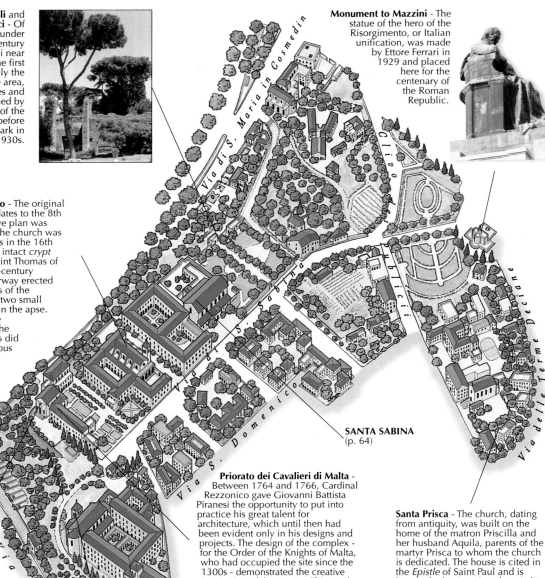

SANTA SABINA
(p. 64)

Priorato dei Cavalieri di Malta - Between 1764 and 1766, Cardinal Rezzonico gave Giovanni Battista Piranesi the opportunity to put into practice his great talent for architecture, which until then had been evident only in his designs and projects. The design of the complex - for the Order of the Knights of Malta, who had occupied the site since the 1300s - demonstrated the creative inspiration of this master. This can be seen in the decorations: stele, obelisks, heraldic emblems, panoplies, and aedicules are integrated with the essential architectural lines, reflecting the neoclassical spirit. The taste for the scenographic arrangement is demonstrated by the *view of the cupola of Saint Peter's*, which can be seen through a keyhole in the main doorway.

Santa Maria del Priorato - In designing this small church, Piranesi combined the most important styles in the religious architecture of Rome: on the one hand, the severity of the **facade**, inspired by the Counter-Reformation, is mixed with ornate decorations, while the interior, with the finely ornamented symbols of the Order of Malta, is a fanciful 17th-century transposition of the stylistic canons of Borromini.

Santa Prisca - The church, dating from antiquity, was built on the home of the matron Priscilla and her husband Aquila, parents of the martyr Prisca to whom the church is dedicated. The house is cited in the *Epistle* of Saint Paul and is known for having given hospitality to Saint Peter. The remains of a *Roman house* are still visible, along with those of a 3rd-century **Mithraeum** containing sections of frescoes related to that Eastern religion. Next to that is the *crypt*, where the relics of the saint are kept. The church was restored several times, shortened and almost rebuilt in 1456 after a partial collapse. The facade was redesigned by Carlo Lambardi in the 17th century. Inside, above the high altar, is the *Baptism of Saint Prisca*, a 17th-century masterpiece by Passignano.

N

Sant'Anselmo - The church, linked to the monastery of the same name, was built in the late 1800s in Romanesque style with a trussed ceiling and mosaic decorations in the apse.

Bastione della Colonnella - Commissioned by Paul III as a reinforcement to the Aurelian walls, the bastion was designed by Antonio da Sangallo the Younger.

The Pyramid of Caius Cestius - This peculiar funerary monument of Gaius Cestius, designed in the likeness of an Egyptian pyramid, was built in 12 BC and ended up within the perimeter of the Aurelian walls 200 years later. The structure, about 36 meters high, is made of mortar covered by blocks of volcanic tufa stone, with a sepulchral chamber inside.

BASILICA DI SAN PAOLO FUORI LE MURA

St. Paul's is the second largest of the four major Jubilee basilicas after St. Peter's and, for that matter, one of the largest churches in the world. Founded under Constantine, the basilica has unfortunately come to us in its modern version following the fire of 1823 that destroyed the original structure and, with it, the Byzantine, Renaissance and Baroque restorations that had characterized the history of the building. The church is preceded by a vast **quadriporticus**, with a statue of St. Paul by the artist Obici at its center. This structure leads into the actual basilica, with its monumental dimensions (132 meters long, 65 meters wide and 30 meters high).

The **nave** is set off by 80 colossal granite columns and is topped by the 19th-century coffered ceiling. A unique mosaic frieze extends to the aisles, with *portraits of the popes*, from St. Peter until modern times, recounting the long history of the Catholic Church. To the right of the main doorway is the 11th-century bronze *Porta Santa*, decorated with *Scenes from the Old and New Testament*, which is opened at the beginning of the Jubilee year.

The 19th-century reconstruction nevertheless contains numerous pieces of the original structure that escaped the flames and were restored. The *triumphal arch* is decorated on one side with splendid mosaics dating to the time of Pope Leo the Great (5th century), portraying *Christ with Two Angels*, the *Symbols of the Evangelists*, and the *24 Elders of the Apocalypse*. The 13th-century mosaics by Pietro Cavallini on the reverse side were once on the facade.

The **apse** is also decorated by a large *mosaic* with at its center the *Blessing Christ*. It is the work of Venetian artists who executed it in the Byzantine style under Pope Honorius III. A short distance ahead, at the edge of the transept and preceded by the confessio, is the *high altar*. Its stupendous *ciborium* is an elegant work in the Gothic style executed in 1285 by Arnolfo da Cambio and a certain Pietro, erroneously confused with Cavallini. To the right of the altar is the *Easter candle*, more than 5 meters high and illustrated by Pietrò Vassalletto and Niccolò d'Angelo in the late 12th century with reliefs portraying human, vegetable and animal motifs mixed with religious scenes.

The **transept**, totally rebuilt in the 19th century, nevertheless contains numerous relics of the Baroque restoration of the basilica, especially in the *Chapels of St. Stephen, of the Crucifix* and *of Saint Laurence*, all designed by

Porta San Paolo - The gate is situated at the beginning of the ancient Via Laurentina and Via Ostiensis, which corresponded to the two original arches still visible from the inside. These were changed into a single arch on the exterior by Honorius. The gate was called Porta Ostiensis in antiquity and owes its present name to the vicinity of the Basilica of San Paolo fuori le Mura. The two heavy semi-circular towers house the **Museo della Via Ostiense**, which contains archaeological findings and models of the ancient road connecting Rome with the port of Ostia.

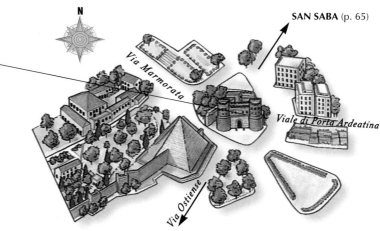

SAN SABA (p. 65)

BASILICA DI SAN PAOLO FUORI LE MURA

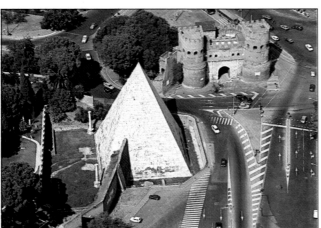

Abbazia delle Tre Fontane - This abbey, on the Via Laurenziana, a short distance from the Basilica di San Paolo fuori le Mura, is a stop of great symbolic and religious importance on the Jubilee route, as it was here that Saint Paul, the Apostle of the Gentiles, was martyred by beheading. Traditionally, when his head fell to the ground it rebounded three times and gave rise to three springs of water. In the 4th century, a chapel in honor of the saint, later to become **San Paolo alle Tre Fontane**, was built near the site. The nearby churches of **Santi Vincenzo e Anastasio** and **Santa Maria Scala Coeli** are of later construction.

San Paolo fuori le Mura.
a general view of the facade and the quadriporticus, the large nave with the frescoed triumphal arch, and a detail of the facade mosaic of the Blessing Christ.

Maderno. Among the interesting works of art found here are a 14th-century *Crucifix* in the second chapel, attributed to Cavallini, whose tomb is also there. Vassalletto, with other Cosmati, was responsible for the **cloister** connected to the basilica. Like the cloister of St. John Lateran, that of St. Paul's displays refined columns in a great variety of forms, with mosaic highlighting. The columns support small arches, above which are set beams decorated with

San Paolo fuori le Mura. The Cosmatesque cloister.

fanciful inlays of polychrome marble and with a mosaic inscription in gold letters on a blue background.
Located in the cloister are the **Sala del Martirologio,** or the Oratory of Saint Julian, the **Baptistery**, the **Sala Gregoriana,** the **Chapel of Reliquaries** and the **Pinacoteca**, with several interesting works of art, including a *Flagellation* by Bramante and a *Crucifix with Saint Brigid* by Cigoli.

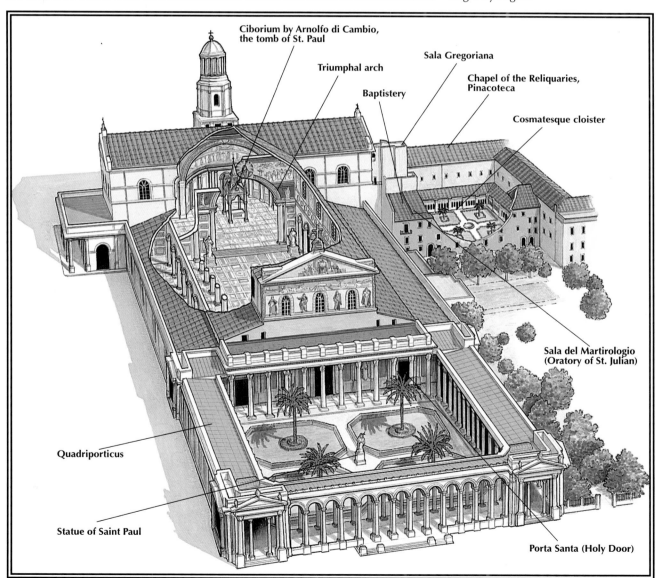

Ciborium by Arnolfo di Cambio, the tomb of St. Paul

Triumphal arch

Sala Gregoriana

Baptistery

Chapel of the Reliquaries, Pinacoteca

Cosmatesque cloister

Sala del Martirologio (Oratory of St. Julian)

Quadriporticus

Statue of Saint Paul

Porta Santa (Holy Door)

Santa Sabina. View of the church, with a section of the right exterior, the interior and, below, the side portico and the exterior of the apse.

SANTA SABINA

The church of Santa Sabina is without a doubt one of the most complete examples of early Christian architecture in Rome. The church was brought back to its primitive splendor in the 1900s with restorations that eliminated several structures added by Domenico Fontana and Francesco Borromini between the late 1500s and the first half of the 1600s. The church was founded in 422 by Peter of Illyria and covered an older building that belonged to a Roman matron named Sabina, then confounded with the Umbrian saint of the same name, for whom the primitive *titulus Sabinae* was built. The adjoining **convent** is linked to the figure of Saint Dominic; in the 13th century, he oversaw the building of the harmonious **cloister**, which looked out at the *chapter house* and the saint's *cell*.

The brick **exterior** of the church has a series of windows with their original *transenna* in selenite, a very fragile building material, while a 15th-century **portico** leads to the atrium, containing architectural fragments from the church brought to light during the 20th-century restoration. The main doorway here, perhaps originally part a building of the Imperial age, holds two very precious 5th-century cypress *doors*. These are decorated with rich frames, bearing animal and flora motifs, that still hold 10 of the 28 original panels depicting *Scenes from the Old and New Testaments*.

The **interior** of the church has a basilica plan with columns setting off the nave from the two aisles. Its form recalls the basilicas of Ravenna, and like them it was decorated with mosaics. Of the original mosaics, however, there remains only a fragment above the door with an inscription commemorat-

San Saba.
The interior and a detail of
the ancient schola
cantorum. *Below, the*
Cosmatesque bishop's
throne.

ing the founding of the church by Peter of Illyria during the pontificate of Caelestunus I, while the two female figures symbolize, respectively, the Church as born from the conversion of Gentiles (*Ecclesia es gentibus*) and as born from the conversion of the Jews (*Ecclesia es circumcisione*). The apsidal mosaics of *Christ Seated among the Apostles* were instead removed and in their place Taddeo Zuccari frescoes on the same theme. A decorative inlay of porphyry and serpentine with motifs symbolizing chalices and crosses runs between the arcades of the **nave**, in the center of which stands the *burial stone of Muñoz de Zamora* (14th century) with the mosaic effigy of the Provincial General of the Dominicans in mosaic. Farther ahead is the *enclosure of the schola cantorum*, dating to the pontificate of Eugenius II (9th century), decorated with Byzantine style elements depicting plants and animals. In the **right aisle** is a curious relic placed atop a small column: a black stone that according to tradition Satan threw at Saint Dominic to break him away from his prayers. A short distance away is a 16th-century *chapel* with frescoes by Zuccari and the Renaissance *funerary monument of Cardinal Auxia*, with its unique Latin inscription, from the school of Andrea Bregno.

SAN SABA

Descending from the summit of the so-called Grande Aventino, and climbing back up the hill known as the Piccolo Aventino, one arrives at the church of San Saba, preceded by a 13th-century Romanesque porch and a large forecourt. The church, dedicated to the monk and saint Sabas who founded the first monastic communities in Asia Minor, was built in the 7th century and largely restructured in the 13th and 15th centuries. The site is also bound to the figure of Saint Sylvia, mother of Saint Gregory the Great, who in the 5th century founded the primitive oratory upon which the present church was built. The last restoration, by Cardinal

Francesco Piccolomini, produced the **portico** and **gallery with loggia** as well as the fresco on the triumphal arch. Under this were found some interesting objects from the Roman and medieval periods, including a fine *sarcophagus* and an 8th century relief depicting a *Horseman with a falcon*. The fine doorway, decorated with refined Cosmatesque mosaic highlights, leads into the rather simple and bare **interior**, curiously divided into a nave and three aisles as a result of incorporating an ancient portico that abutted on the left aisle. The original nave and aisles, each of which terminates in an apse, contain numerous works that testify to the building's medieval past, such as the *bishop's throne*, the *high altar*, and the remains of the *ambones* (pulpits) and of the *schola cantorum*, standing side by side in the right aisle. The primitive mosaic decorations have mostly disappeared and been replaced by *frescoes*, some of which, dating from the 13th century, are from the Subiaco school.

Some *fragments of wall paintings* (7th-9th centuries) from the church and the fortified convent that rose next to it are exhibited in the corridor of the *sacristy*, where the entrance to the *subterranean oratory* founded by St. Sylvia is located.

Porta San Sebastiano - Originally called Porta Appia, the gate was built by Aurelius in connection with the consular Via Appia, with an opening of two arches and with cylindrical towers on each side. Honorius had the towers raised a further two storeys and strengthened with a robust quadrangular base. With only one of the two arches remaining, the exterior was restored with marble taken from the burial monuments lining the first section of the road. The gate, which is the best preserved of the Aurelian walls, houses the **Museum of the Roman Walls**.

San Giovanni a Porta Latina - Probably founded around the 5th century, the church has undergone significant changes over the course of the centuries. It nevertheless still maintains much of its medieval appearance, with the facade featuring marble and granite columns and a beautiful 12th-century Romanesque *campanile*. The interior, with marble columns of varying dimensions separating the nave and aisles, contains a **cycle of frescoes** from the 12th century with *Scenes from the Old and New Testaments*.

Arch of Drusus - The arch was erected between 211 and 216 to allow for the passage of the *Aqua Antoniniana*, the branch of the aqueduct that fed the nearby Baths of Caracalla, above the Via Appia. Honorius made it part of the defensive system of the adjoining Porta San Sebastiano, maintaining the fine columns in ancient yellow marble which can still be admired.

San Giovanni in Oleo - This small 5th-century oratory, completely rebuilt under Julius II by Baldassarre Peruzzi and later renovated by Borromini in 1658, was erected on the spot where Saint John the Evangelist was martyred. Its name is derived from the cauldron of boiling oil in which the saint was said to have been immersed and from which he came out unharmed.

Tomb of Priscilla - The tomb, built by the freeman Domitian Abascanthus for his wife Priscilla, was an enormous cylindrical mound covered in travertine and decorated with niches and statues. The Caetani erected a guard tower on the tomb in the 13th century, the remains of which are still visible. The **Catacombs of Priscilla** are located on the Via Salaria.

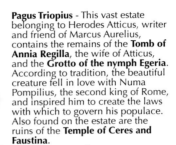

Porta Latina - Flanked by a medieval tower, this gate is built of travertine and represents one the best preserved sections of the Aurelian Walls.

Pagus Triopius - This vast estate belonging to Herodes Atticus, writer and friend of Marcus Aurelius, contains the remains of the **Tomb of Annia Regilla**, the wife of Atticus, and the **Grotto of the nymph Egeria**. According to tradition, the beautiful creature fell in love with Numa Pompilius, the second king of Rome, and inspired him to create the laws with which to govern his populace. Also found on the estate are the ruins of the **Temple of Ceres and Faustina**.

Jewish Catacombs - Together with those of the Villa Torlonia, these catacombs constitute the largest underground cemetery of the Roman Jewish community in the Imperial age.

BASILICA DI SAN SEBASTIANO

Via Appia

CATACOMBS OF DOMITILLA
(p. 68)

CATACOMBS OF SAN CALLISTO
(p. 68)

CATACOMBS OF SAN SEBASTIANO
(p. 68)

Via Ardeatina

Church of 'Domine quo vadis?' - Known in the Middle Ages as Santa Maria in Palmis, or del Passo, the church was built in the 9th century and again rebuilt between the 1500s and 1600s on the site where, according to tradition, Christ appeared to St. Peter as he was fleeing Rome; upon being asked the fateful question *"Domine, quo vadis?"* (Lord, whither goest thou?), Christ answered *"Romam iterum crucifigi"* (To Rome, to be crucified again). With that, the Apostle returned to Rome to face his martyrdom. The stone on which Jesus left his imprint (thus the medieval name of the church) was preserved here before being moved to the basilica of San Sebastiano.

THE CONSULAR ROADS

The Romans were the greatest road builders of antiquity. The most tangible sign of Roman expansion, the road network expanded apace with their territorial conquests and allowed for relatively easy linkages with the capital. First laid out during the Republican age and then lengthened during the Imperial age, the so-called 'consular roads' radiated from the center of Rome. They began, or converged, in the Roman Forum at the *Miliarium aureum*, a column erected by Augustus with the distances between Rome and the most important cities of the Empire inscribed on it. The first of the Roman roads was the Via **Appia Antica** (Appian Way), begun in 312 BC by the censor Appius Claudius. The road left Rome through the ancient Porta Capena in the Servian walls (and later through Porta San Sebastiano in the Aurelian walls), and ran almost 400 kilometers to the city of Brindisi (Brundusium), is southern Italy. Running north, instead, was the Via **Flaminia**, built between 223 and 219 BC by the censor Gaius Flaminius and linking the city with Rimini. The road, passing through the Aurelian walls at Porta Flaminia (now Porta del Popolo), crossed the Tiber at Ponte Milivio (*Pons Milvius*). This was also the point of departure for another north-running road, the Via **Cassia**, built between 117 and 107 BC by censor Lucius Cassius Longinus to link Rome with central Etruria. The Cassia linked up to the Via **Aurelia**, opened in 241 by censor Gaius Aurelius. Leaving Rome from the Porta Aurelia (now Porta San Pancrazio), the road connected Rome to the Tyrrhenian coast. Extended during the imperial age to Arles, in France, the Aurelia rejoined the Cassia near Luni, near present-day La Spezia, and was throughout the Middle Ages the main link with France, taking on the name 'Francigena' and becoming the route used by pilgrims coming to Rome from northern Europe.

Tomb of Cecilia Metella - Symbol of the Appian Way, this tomb, remaining nearly intact with the addition of the crenellated tower installed by the Caetani family in 1302 when it was made the keep for their adjacent castle, is the best preserved piece of the entire archaeological park. The tomb was erected around 50 BC for Cecilia Metella, the daughter of the counsel Quintus Metellus Creticus and the wife of the son of Crassus, a member of the first triumvirate with Caesar and Pompey. At one time the tumulus, 20 meters in diameter, had a conical covering that was subsequently demolished. Still intact is the frieze with bucrania–heads of oxen garlanded with flowers–which gave rise to the area being called *Capo di Bove*. Next to the picturesque remains of the 14th-century **Caetani Castle** are the ruins of the antique Gothic church of **San Nicola a Capo di Bove**, a rare example of this style of architectural in Rome.

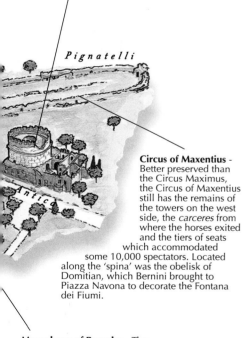

Pignatelli

Circus of Maxentius - Better preserved than the Circus Maximus, the Circus of Maxentius still has the remains of the towers on the west side, the *carceres* from where the horses exited and the tiers of seats which accommodated some 10,000 spectators. Located along the 'spina' was the obelisk of Domitian, which Bernini brought to Piazza Navona to decorate the Fontana dei Fiumi.

Mausoleum of Romulus - The structure, built by Maxentius for his young son Romulus, consisted of a large area enclosed by a portico, with a cylindrical building rising at the center. Inside, placed within the central pilaster, were the niches for the cinerary urns.

BASILICA DI SAN SEBASTIANO

Built as the *Basilica Apostolorum* where the bodies of Saints Peter and Paul were once kept temporarily, the church, one of the seven pilgrimage churches of Rome, was dedicated to Saint Sebastian in the middle of the 4th century. The saint's relics had been placed in the crypt below. In the early 1600s, Cardinal Scipione Borghese asked Flaminio Ponzio to rebuild the church, which was later completed by Vesanzio, giving it an elegant **facade** with a portico and an **interior** with a single nave and a fine wooden ceiling. The church contains the **Chapel of the Relics**, with the original stone bearing the footprints of Christ from '*Domine, quo vadis?*' The other chapel, dedicated to Saint Sebastian, holds one of the arrows shot into the saint and is built above his crypt. There is also a *statue of the saint* by Giorgetti, a pupil of Bernini.

Basilica of Saint Sebastian. The interior and the facade.

Right, a detail of the wooden ceiling with an image of the martyr Saint Sebastian.

The Catacombs of San Callisto. The painting of the Good Shepherd in the Crypt of Lucina and a view of the Crypt of Saint Cecilia.

THE CATACOMBS

CATACOMBS OF SAN SEBASTIANO

Dug out of an ancient stone quarry, the catacombs of San Sebastiano were initially a pagan burial ground before being used by Christians. They were actually composed of three **mausoleums**, built in the 2nd century and covered with earth a century later to create an open flat area, the so-called **Triclia**, with a portico where the *refrigeria*, or liturgical banquets, were held and where the relics of Saints Peter and Paul, brought here temporarily in 258, were worshipped. The central focus of the intricate labyrinth of galleries is the **Crypt of Saint Sebastian**, where the martyr who gave his name to the entire burial grounds was entombed. The numerous rooms of the catacombs have extremely interesting frescoes. Worthy of note among them is the fresco in the **Cubiculum of Jonah**, with a cycle depicting the famous biblical figure, and the *Miracle of the Demoniac of Gerasa*, preserved in one of the three mausoleums. The subterranean grounds also contain the remains of the *Basilica Apostolorum*.

CATACOMBS OF SAN CALLISTO

These vast catacombs, spreading out over four levels with some 20 kilometers of galleries, display an immense number of *cubicula* and *hypogea* decorated with frescoes in the preserved areas. The most ancient nuclei are the **Papal Crypt**, where the popes who were martyred and sanctified in the first centuries of Christianity were buried; the **Crypt of Santa Cecilia**, where the body of the young martyr was found; the **Crypt of Lucina;** and the **Cubicula of the Sacraments**, with 3rd-century frescoes representing a wide range of religious subjects. Dating from the 4th century are the **Crypts of Saints Gaius and Eusebius**, with the *sarcophagi* of the two popes.

CATACOMBS OF DOMITILLA

The catacombs, also called the Catacombs of saints Nereus and Achilleus, are among the largest in Rome. According to tradition, they were built from the simple household sepulcher that belonged to Domitilla, the wife and niece of Flavius Clement and put to death by Domitian.

Inside of the catacombs are the remains of the **Basilica of Santi Nereo e Achilleo**; behind the apse is a cubiculum containing the fresco of *The Defunct Venerable Invoking St. Petronilla*. Near the basilica is the very ancient *Cemetery of the Flavians*.

Another area of the catacombs is the so-called 'Good Shepherd', which preserves 2nd-century AD paintings in the vault. Found in a later area are fine depictions of the grain market and scenes of everyday work (3rd-4th century).

Catacombs of Domitilla. The Basilica of Santi Nereo e Achilleo.

THE CHURCHES OF ROME

**SANT' AGNESE
IN AGONE**

**SANTA MARIA
IN COSMEDIN**

**SANTA MARIA
DELLA VITTORIA**

**SANTA CECILIA
IN TRASTEVERE**

**SANTA FRANCESCA
ROMANA**

**SANTI DOMENICO
E SISTO**

**SANTA MARIA
DELL'ORTO**

**SAN CARLINO ALLE
QUATTRO FONTANE**

**TRINITÀ
DEI MONTI**

**SAN PIETRO IN
MONTORIO**

The interior of San Giorgio in Velabro, with the splendid Cosmatesque ciborium; below, two details of the fresco in the apse of the Virgin with Saints George, Peter, and Sebastian.

SAN GIORGIO IN VELABRO

This church, built probably in the 6th century near the *Velabrum*, the marsh where according to legend Romulus and Remus were found, was initially dedicated to Saints George and Sebastian, the patrons of the cavalry and of weapons.

The name of the former titulary took root in common usage when Pope Zachary brought the head of the saint here as a relic. In the ninth century, under Pope Gregory IV, the church was partially reconstructed in Romanesque style: the side naves were added and the apse and the presbytery, in which a stupendous Cosmatesque **ciborium** was installed, were remodeled.

New modifications to the original structure came about in the 12th century with the addition of the Ionic **portico** and the **bell tower**.

The vault of the apse was decorated near the end of the following century with frescoes of *Christ, the Virgin, and Saints George, Peter, and Sebastian* that are attributed to Pietro Cavallini but are more probably the work of his pupils.

SAN GIOVANNI DECOLLATO

The Confraternita di San Giovanni Decollato (Confraternity of Saint John the Beheaded) was founded in 1488 with the support of the Florentine city-state; the task of the brothers was to provide spiritual and material assistance to those condemned to death. The area of the ancient church of Santa Maria de Fovea was chosen to provide the sodality with an appropriate place of worship, and in the early 1500s, construction of a new complex dedicated to Saint John, the patron saint of Florence, was begun.

The church, with its *oratory* and the adjacent *cloister* and *cemetery* where the bodies of the executed were buried, was completed halfway through the century. The buildings are fully Counter-Reformist in spirit and represent an excellent expression of full-blown Roman Mannerism, especially in the interior decoration. The ornamentation of the church is the result of a harmonious mix of *stuccowork*, *inlays*, and *marbles* that provide a fitting frame for the many frescoes by artists of the caliber of Zucchi, Vasari, and Pomarancio.

The oratory, which includes the *Camera Storica della Confraternita* with its collection of the instruments used in meting out capital punishment, is richly decorated with frescoes of the Tuscan Mannerist school.

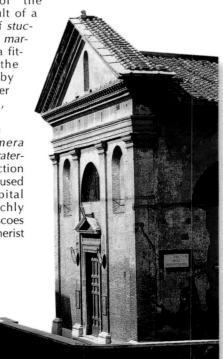

San Giovanni Decollato. The monumental facade.

SANTA MARIA IN COSMEDIN

When, in the late 19th century, Sardi's beautiful Baroque facade was demolished, the church of Santa Maria in
Cosmedin rediscovered its early medieval aspect. This is in
fact the period (6th-7th century) in which the original building was raised on the ruins of the Roman *Annona* - the offices superintending the Forum Boarium and other trade forums - and of the 5th-century BC temple of Ceres with the
conjoined *Ara Maxima*, from the structure of which the crypt
of the church is said to have been created. About two centuries after its construction, Pope
Hadrian I commissioned
some decorative work
(hence the appellative
'Cosmedin') and do-
nated the building
to the Greek friars
who had es-
caped the ico-
noclastic perse-
cutions that rav-
aged the Byzan-
tine east. Fur-
ther work was
carried out under
Pope Calixtus II
during the first
quarter of the 12th
century, when the
graceful Romanesque **bell
tower,** with its several orders
of windows, and the portico were
built. The portico shelters the celebrated **Bocca della Verità**, a
Roman drain cover in the form of the mask of a river god that
according to medieval tradition would 'bite' anyone who
dared tell a lie with his hand inserted between the jaws.
In the highly evocative **interior**, besides the iconostasis and
the frescoes in the apse, which were substantially retouched
in the nineteenth century, are one of the most beautiful cosmatesque *floors* in Rome and an elegant *Gothic ciborium*, a
late 14th-century work by Deodatus of Cosma.
The neoclassical **sacristy** is instead the setting for a precious
and brilliantly-colored gold-
ground mosaic depiction of
the *Epiphany*. It is actually
a fragment of an 8th-cen-
tury work of much greater
size from the Chapel of
John VII in the ancient
Vatican Basilica.

*Santa Maria in Cosmedin. The Bocca della Verità under
the portico and an aisle; below, a detail of the mosaic
of the Epiphany in the sacristy and a detail of the
Cosmati work floor.*

SAN GIUSEPPE DEI FALEGNAMI AND THE MAMERTINE PRISON

The church, placed in the care of the Confraternity of Carpenters, was built during the reign of Pope Paul III, beginning in 1597, in a style that marks the transition from the severe lines of Counter-Reformist architecture to the more decorative Baroque style. The interior gives access to the adjacent oratory with its beautiful decorations in purest Mannerist style. Underneath the church are two rooms of the ancient **Mamertine Prison**, which by medieval tradition was the site of the confinement of Saint Peter. It is said that before his escape, the saint used the water that miraculously gushed forth from the pavement to baptize the two guardians Processo and Martiniano.

The column to which the chains, today preserved in San Pietro in Vincoli, bound the first pope of the Christian Church has been venerated as a relic since the 15th century. Although the tradition would seem to have no historical foundation, the site remains one of the salient points in the pilgrimages of the faithful to Rome. The *lower* cell of the prison, probably originally a cistern, is the oldest part and in all likelihood was part of the original Tullianum Prison; the *upper* cell, trapezoidal in form, was built in 40 BC by the consuls Caius Vibius Rufinus and Marcus Cocceius Nerva, to whom we also owe the travertine **facade**. Some of Rome's most famous enemies, including Jugurtha and Vercingetorix, met their deaths in this prison.

SANTA MARIA ANTIQUA

Together with the **Oratorio dei Quaranta Martiri**, this church occupies a building of the imperial era traditionally denominated the **Temple of Augustus** at the corner of the Forum with the Palatine. Originally, the church was an early Christian basilica with a nave and two aisles built according to Byzantine canons, with an atrium and a narthex, on the ruins of which Santa Maria Liberatrice rose in the eighth century. This second church was rebuilt in the 17th century but demolished in the 20th to again bring to light the remains of the Santa Maria Antiqua we see today. The church still conserves precious frescoes from all the different eras in which the building was remodeled and redecorated. Among the most important is an 8th-century *Crucifixion* in the to the left chapel of the apse, in which the typical iconographic scheme of the evangelical episode, which over the centuries became tradition and has been repeated in innumerable versions, is already firmly established: Saint John and the Virgin at the foot of the Cross, the soldier Longinus piercing Christ's side with his lance, and the other soldier offering Him the sponge soaked in bile.

The interior of the Mamertine Prison under the church of San Giuseppe dei Falegnami, with on the left the column to which Saint Peter was reputedly chained.

A detail of the frescoes in the church of Santa Maria Antiqua.

The Temple of the Divus Romulus that forms the atrium of the church of Santi Cosma e Damiano. Two small porphyry columns frame the original bronze portal on the curvilinear exterior.

SANTI COSMA E DAMIANO

The church was built on the remains of two buildings of the imperial age, the **Temple of the Divus Romulus**, which became the atrium, and the *Biblioteca Pacis*, the remains of which are still visible. The **interior**, with the entrance on Via dei Fori Imperiali, was completely restructured in the 17th century by Bernini's pupil Arrigucci, who also created the adjacent **cloister**.

Despite its new Baroque raiment, including the beautiful gilded and painted wooden ceiling decorated by Mantegna with *Saints Cosmas and Damian in Glory*, testimony to the original appearance of the church is borne by the beautiful **mosaics** from the 6th-7th centuries that adorn the apsidal portion of the building and that were taken as a model for many later mosaic decorations in Rome. In the *Christ with Saints Peter, Paul, Cosmas, Damian, and Theodore and Pope Felix IV* that adorns the apsidal vault, the pope is carrying the model of the church, which he had built in about 530; on the triumphal arch are instead portrayed the *Apocalypse with the Mystical Lamb, Saints, and the Symbols of the Evangelists Luke and John* and, below, the *Elders of the Apocalypse*.

SAN LORENZO IN MIRANDA

The site of the ancient **Temple of Antoninus and Faustina**, of which many significant remains are still visible, was once occupied by a church built in the 7th-8th centuries and completely restructured on occasion of Charles V's visit to Rome in 1528. Part of the work involved freeing the pronaos of the temple from the medieval superstructures and consequently reducing the size of the church, which was again remodeled by Torriani in the early 17th century. The entrance to the church is on Via dei Fori Imperiali; it is presently under the patronage of the Collegio Chimico Farmaceutico, the successor to that Collegio degli Speziali that was made titular in 1430 by Pope Martin V. In the interior, on the main altar, is the *Martyrdom of Saint Laurence* by Pietro da Cortona.

SANTI LUCA E MARTINA

Elegant, harmonious forms, a tall, graceful dome, and a marvelous **facade**, a masterpiece by Pietro da Cortona who was buried here with his family members, characterize this building of ancient foundation. In 1588, Pope Sixtus V granted the premises to the Accademia del Disegno di San Luca; Saint Luke the Evangelist thus became co-titular of the church with the early Christian Saint Martina. The academy, which stood facing the church itself, was demolished during the work for opening the route of what is today Via dei Fori Imperiali and transferred to its present home in Palazzo Carpegna in the Trevi district. In the interior of *lower* church are valuable works by da Cortona and Algardi; the balanced volumes of the *upper* church, on a Greek cross plan, are abundantly and richly decorated.

The Temple of Antoninus and Faustina with the church of San Lorenzo in Miranda.

Santi Luca e Martina. The lovely facade by Pietro da Cortona.

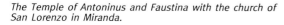

SANTA FRANCESCA ROMANA

Despite its original dedication to Santa Maria *Nova* in counterpoint to the other forum church named after Saint Mary, with the appellative *Antiqua*, this church, which rose in the ninth century near the **Temple of Venus and Rome**, is commonly known as Santa Francesca Romana, a saint much venerated by the Romans and buried in the **crypt**. The **facade** is the work of Carlo Lambardi (1615). The soaring, five-story **bell tower**, with inlays in majolica tile and porphyry crosses, instead dates to the 12th century.

In the **interior**, alongside highly valuable works of art, is an important and we might say 'curious' relic: the so-called *Silices Apostolici*, stones said to conserve the footprints of Saint Peter and linked to the story of Simon Magus, who offered the saint money in exchange for the power to give the Holy Ghost with the laying-on of his hands (whence the term 'simony' for the sale of a church office or ecclesiastical preferment). Among the church's works of art are the apsidal **mosaics**, in imitation Byzantine style although dating to the 12th century, portraying the *Virgin with the Child and Saints*; the precious icon of the *Glycophilusa Madonna*, a 5th-century work moved here from Santa Maria Antiqua; and the two interesting *funeral monuments*. One is that dedicated to Pope Gregory XI, who died in 1378 after his return to Rome at the end of the exile of the papacy in Avignon. The other is to Antonio da Rio, the warden of Castel Sant'Angelo during the first half of the Quattrocento, here portrayed on horseback; this is the only example of this type of portraiture in any church in Rome.

SANTA MARIA DI LORETO

In this typical example of a central-plan church there coexist two different currents in 16th-century Roman architecture, one inspired by Bramantesque classicism and more firmly anchored in the Renaissance stylistic models, the other of Michelangelesque inspiration, thoroughly Mannerist in style and already looking ahead to the triumph of the Baroque.

The building - raised on the site of the Temple of the Divus Trajanus - was begun in 1507 by Antonio da Sangallo the Younger, who built the square brick base with travertine pilaster strips, probably to a design by Bramante.

The church was completed less than eighty years later by Jacopo Del Duca, a gifted pupil of Michelangelo, who added both the grandiose octagonal **dome,** topped by its unconventional *lantern*, and the *bell tower*; he also laid out the decorative scheme for the octagonal interior, with chapels in the ample niches, which was later adorned with stuccowork, frescoes, and sculptures, of note among which are the two *Angels* by Maderno and the vivid *Saint Susanna*, a 17th-century work by Duquesnoy.

The facade of Santa Francesca Romana.

The church of the Santissimo Nome di Maria, right, copies the central-plan domed structure of the adjacent Santa Maria di Loreto, left.

SANTISSIMO NOME DI MARIA

In a certain sense, this building is the reinterpretation, in a late-Baroque key, of the adjacent church of Santa Maria di Loreto, of which it copies the central plan structure and the domed roof. Work on this church, which began in 1736 under the supervision of Antoine Dérizet, continued under Mauro Fontana, also the author of the beautiful high altar in polychrome marbles on which stands an ancient image of the *Virgin* (13th century) originally in the Lateran oratory. The church owes its name to the Confraternita del Santissimo Nome di Maria, which commissioned its construction to commemorate Sobiesky's victory over the Turks in 1683.

SANTI DOMENICO E SISTO

This church, managed by the Dominican friars and also called San Sisto Nuovo, arose in the 16th century on the ancient Santa Maria a Magnanapoli.
The new single-nave building was begun by Giacomo Della Porta; it was restored under Urban VIII and completed by the addition of the theatrical Baroque **facade**, which, with the **staircase**, would seem to be the work of Vincenzo Della Greca, who also placed Maderno's statues of *Saint Thomas Aquinas* and *Saint Peter Martyr* in the lower niches (those of the upper niches, of the titular saints of the church, are by Canini). The **interior** space is as if dilated by the prospective fresco of the *Apotheosis of Saint Dominic*, a 17th-century work by Domenico Maria Canuti and Enrico Haffner, and is further embellished by the sculptural group entitled *Noli me tangere* by Antonio Raggi and an excellent high altar built to designs by Gian Lorenzo Bernini.

The facade of the church of Santi Domenico e Sisto with its theatrical staircase.

San Pietro in Vincoli. The chains that reputedly bound the apostle Peter. Below, the facade of the church with the 15th-century portico.

SAN PIETRO IN VINCOLI

This church, one of the most venerated minor basilicas in Rome, is named for the first pope of the Roman Church. It is also called the Basilica Eudoxiana, after emperor Valentinian III's wife, who received from her mother the **chains** that bound Saint Peter in Jerusalem and donated them to Pope Leo I. When set together with those that had bound the Apostle in Rome's Mamertine Prison, they united to form a single piece. The relic is still kept here and the old Latin name *in vinculis* has remained.
Built on an ancient site of Christian worship, the basilica was consecrated by Pope Sixtus III in 439 AD. Despite medieval and Renaissance restoration, the early Christian plan is still evident in the length of the nave, typical of the period, and in the rows of white marble Ionic **columns** separating the nave and aisles. The arcades of the **portico** before the entrance, built in the 1400s by Baccio Pontelli or Meo del Caprino, are supported by octagonal pilasters. The **interior** is the result of 18th-century restorations by Francesco Fontana, who also designed the wooden ceiling decorated by the *Miracle of the Chains* by Parodi.

In the right transept is the unfinished **Mausoleum of Julius II** by Michelangelo. The grandiose funeral monument was conceived by the Tuscan master as a colossal mausoleum adorned with some 40 statues and numerous reliefs and was to have been placed beneath the cupola of St. Peter's. Begun in 1513, the work was halted three years later and was never taken up again; the completed pieces were later assembled with the imposing figure of Michelangelo's **Moses** in the center. Flanking Moses are the statues of Leah and Rachel begun by Michelangelo and finished by his pupil Raffaello da Montelupo. Other of his pupils executed the *Effigy of the Pope*, the *Virgin and Child*, a *Prophet*, and a *Sibyl*. Also in the church are the so-called *sarcophagus of the Maccabee brothers*, kept in the **crypt**, the fine 7th-century Byzantine mosaic of *St. Sebastian*, and the tombs of *Nicola Cusano* and of *Antonio and Piero del Pollaiolo*.

SAN CLEMENTE

One of the oldest churches in Rome, San Clemente is unique for its structure of two superimposed churches sitting atop vast subterranean grounds containing the remains of imperial **Roman buildings** and of a **Mithraic temple** from the 3rd century AD.

One of these buildings was probably the house of Clement, a freedman martyred under Domitian whose relics were kept in the church built in his honor in the 4th century. This original church constitutes the **lower basilica**, an important place of worship during the high Middle Ages and the site of many ecclesiastical councils. The lower basilica, with its central nave and two aisles, is preceded by an atrium and a narthex, both of which are **frescoed**. The **narthex** contains 11th-century wall paintings of the *Miracle of Saint Clement*, with a naive but suggestive depiction of sea creatures, the *Translation of Saint Cyril's Body* and *Saint Cyril in Glory*. The frescoes in the nave and aisles of the church are from the same period. The nave contains the *Legend of Saint Alexis*, who, after leaving his family to become a hermit, returned as a servant, sleeping for years under a staircase and revealing his true identity only at the point of death. Other important frescoes include the *Legend of Saint Clement*, in which the saint is depicted while he celebrates mass in the catacombs. The soldiers who surprise the saint and his faithful are blinded, and instead of carrying off Clement, they take a column.

The **upper basilica**, built by Paschal II after the original church was sacked by the Normans in 1084 and buried, shows strong contrasts with the lower church, with its rich decorations by Carlo Stefano Fontana in the most sumptuous Baroque style of the 1700s. The original structure has nevertheless survived in numerous instances. The *schola cantorum*, for example, preserves its white marble surface, some of it dating from the 12th century and some of it taken from the lower church. While the lower basilica is adorned with frescoes, here **Cosmatesque mosaics** dominate in the fine pavement, the candelabrum, the ambones, the ciborium, and the tabernacle in the high altar, dating from 1299. Particularly noteworthy are the works by the Cosmati in the **apse**, hardly altered from the 12th century, with the long marble bench interrupted by the bishop's throne decorated with mosaic highlighting. On the apse vault, above a frescoed strip, are mosaics of the *Lamb of God with the Twelve Companions* and the *Triumph of the Cross*.

A superb example of the Renaissance restoration is the **Chapel of Saint Catherine**, with its beautiful frescoes from the late 1420s. These are attributed to Masolino da Panicale, the teacher of Masaccio, who perhaps contributed to the work. The most important scenes depict the *Crucifixion* and the *Story of Saint Catherine*.

San Pietro in Vincoli. Moses *by Michelangelo.*

San Clemente.
The interior of the upper basilica with the elegant Cosmatesque pavement in the foreground and the schola cantorum, *in the background the ciborium and the splendid apsidal mosaics of the* Triumph of the Cross *(12th century).*

The upper basilica, Chapel of Saint Catherine. The fresco of the Crucifixion *(15th century).*

The mithraeum (3rd century) of the original lower basilica.

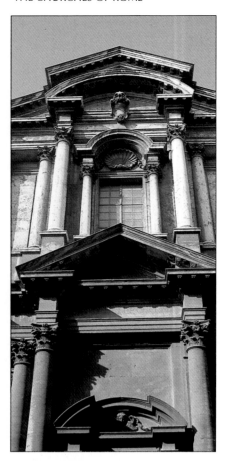

SANTA MARIA IN CAMPITELLI

This is one of Carlo Rainaldi's most interesting architectural creations, built beginning in 1662 and completed five years later. It was built to house the venerated image of the Virgin that saved the city from a serious epidemic in 1656 and replaced an earlier church a short distance away on the site of Palazzo Lovatelli.
Rainaldi applied a genial perspective play both on the **facade**, made especially lively by the elegant arrangement of the columns, and in the **interior**, which repeats the theatrical exterior structure with protruding columns and cornices at the points of encounter of the nave with the transept and with the elongated apse, over which towers the congenial **dome**. The interior perspective is heightened by the sumptuous **high altar** designed by Rainaldi himself and built by De Rossi, in collaboration with Ercole Ferrata and Schor, in 1667. At its center stands the miraculous icon of the *Virgin of the Church of Santa Maria in Portico*, an 11th-century work in enameled metal.
The Chapel of the Relics contains venerated and precious liturgical objects, including the12th-century Byzantine altar of Saint Gregory Nazienzen, decorated with precious mosaics. The fine paintings in the church include a *Virgin with Saint Joachim and Saint Anne* by Luca Giordano and Baciccia's *Nativity of Saint John the Baptist.*

SANTA CATERINA DEI FUNARI

The date of reconstruction of this church on the site of the earlier Santa Maria Dominae Rosae, and that is 1560-1564, would place it in the Counter-Reformist class, although the architecture of the building is actually more directly inspired by the classical forms of the Renaissance; for example, the well-balanced travertine **facade** by Guidetto Guidetti of Como. Of the same period is the bizarre **bell tower**, created by raising the belfry, with its unusual but gracious octagonal dome, on an earlier structure. The organization of the single-nave **interior** that belies the typical late Renaissance taste for a certain severity in form and ornament stands in counterpoint to a cohesive and quite interesting collection of paintings, all dating to only slightly later than the church itself, by some of the most talented masters of the era: Annibale Carracci, Federico Zuccari, Raffaellino da Reggio, and Girolamo Muziano.

SAN NICOLA IN CARCERE

This church, founded certainly before the year 1000 and according to some experts dating to the 7th century, is emblematic of the history of the district and, in a certain sense, of Rome itself, in which almost every monument is the result of the superposition of different eras and styles. In this case, the medieval walls enclose the remains of three republican-era temples of the Forum Holitorium rebuilt in the 1st century AD and contain architectural elements of the most disparate eras. To the north was the **Temple of Spes** (Hope), built following the First Punic War: a line of eight of its columns encased in the side of the church is interrupted by a beautiful Gothic portal. At the center was the **Temple of Juno Sospita**, two columns of which were used for the facade of the church, built in 1599 by Giacomo Della Porta. The structure to the south, dating to 260 BC, was probably the **Temple of Janus**: six of its travertine columns are incorporated in the left wall of the church. The late-Romanesque **bell tower** exploits a pre-existing defensive tower raised in the early Middle Ages by one of the powerful Roman families that controlled the area. The **interior**, on a basilica plan, is also adorned with reused columns and capitals; some of the temple structures visible on the outside of the church penetrate to the interior side walls. Among the many pictorial works are the frescoes by Giovanni Baglione in the Aldobrandini Chapel and the *Virgin with Child* by Antoniazzo Romano, dated to about 1470.

The facade of the church of Santa Maria in Campitelli has many tympana of the most varied forms.

San Nicola in Carcere. The facade of the church and the Roman columns along the right side.

*Michelangelo's Porta Pia.
The side facing the city.*

*Top right, Santa Maria della
Vittoria. The 17th-century facade
and, middle, the statue of Saint
Theresa by Bernini.*

*Bottom, the interior of the
church of Santa Maria degli
Angeli, built out of several
imposing sections of the Baths
of Diocletian.*

SANTA MARIA DELLA VITTORIA

Begun by Maderno in 1608, the church replaced the previous chapel of the convent of the Discalced Carmelites and was supposed to be dedicated to St. Paul by Cardinal Scipione Borghese, who had paid for its construction.

But the 1620 victory in Prague against the Protestants by the Catholic armies led by Ferdinand II of the Habsburg, with the help of an image of the Virgin found near the castle of Pilsen and brought to the still unfinished church, led to the name being changed to Santa Maria della Vittoria. Six years later the church was completed with the **facade** designed by Giovanni Battista Storia.

The **interior**, with a single nave featuring a cupola without a drum, was decorated according to the then prevailing Baroque taste. Contributing to the richness are also paintings by Domenichino, his last ones in Rome, located in the second chapel on the right side and portraying the figure of *Saint Francis*. There is also a *Saint Paul* painted by Gherardo Delle Notti in 1620.

But the masterpiece of this church is in the Cornaro Chapel: the **Saint Theresa** by Bernini. This work depicts the saint in mystic ecstasy transfixed by an angel, while looking on from several niches, as from theater boxes, are the members of the Cornaro family dressed in their 17th-century finery.

SANTA MARIA DEGLI ANGELI

It was a simple priest, Antonio del Duca, who first had the idea of transforming the monumental Baths of Diocletian into a church glorifying the angels and saints who, according to tradition, were forced to build them. The idea came to the attention of Pius IV, who in 1561 gave the job to Michelangelo. The master began work enthusiastically, but did not live to complete it: his salvage of the ruins thus represents the architectural equivalent of the 'unfinished' found in many of his sculptures. Jacopo Del Duca finished transforming the ancient *Tepidarium* and the spaces opening off of its four sides into a church on a Greek-cross plan with three entrances. The Carthusians, who were to receive the church by Pius IV, oversaw the construction of the **convent** (now the Epigraphic Section of the **Museo Nazionale Romano**), whose **cloister** was also based on a design by the Tuscan master.

Two of the three entrances were closed with the construction of the chapels of St. Bruno and Beato Albergati in the 1700s, while Luigi Vanvitelli's remodeled interior for the 1750 Jubilee had new columns set in the recesses leading to the vestibule, aligned with the remaining entrance. These added to the 14-meter high monolithic red granite columns of the **cross nave**, where numerous *altar pieces* from the Saint Peter's Basilica were placed. Other paintings include the *Martyrdom of Saint Sebastian* by Domenichino and the *Baptism of Jesus* by Maratta (whose tomb is located in the vestibule), both in the presbytery, and the *Mass of Saint Basil* by Subleyars, in the left transept.

Santa Maria del Popolo, Chigi Chapel.
Jonah and the Whale *by Lorenzetto and the spired bell tower and the octagonal dome, examples of the Lombard Renaissance style in Rome.*

Santa Maria in Vallicella, also known as Chiesa Nuova.
A detail of the facade, inspired by that of the neighboring Church of Gesù.

San Giovanni dei Fiorentini. *A partial view of the travertine facade crowned with statues.*

SANTA MARIA DEL POPOLO

An outstanding example of Roman Renaissance religious architecture, the church of Santa Maria del Popolo was totally rebuilt by order of Pope Sixtus IV in 1472-1477 on an 11th-century building erected by Pope Paschal II in gratitude to the Virgin for having interceded, in 1096, in the liberation of the Holy Sepulcher. The first construction was financed by the people of Rome; hence the name by which the church is known today. But another, more evocative legend relates that it was built with the declared aim of driving out Nero's ghost, which hovered near one of the poplar trees (in Latin, *populus*) in which the area abounded, near which was laid the first stone of the building. There is some truth in the second version, since the site on which the church now rises was that of the Mausoleum of the Domizii, where the notorious emperor was buried.

The medieval building, which passed, with the adjoining convent, to the Augustinians in the 13th century and then to the Lombard Congregation, was reconstructed by Andrea Bregno and his followers in accordance with the dictates of the Po Valley religious architecture of the time. This style is clearly evinced by the brick **bell tower** with its typically Lombard forms, and the octagonal **dome**, the first of this type to have been built in Rome. In the early Cinquecento, under Pope Julius II, Bramante somewhat modified the 15th-century structure: he remodeled the choir and built the Chigi Chapel to Raphael's designs. About a century later, Bernini

modified the Renaissance structure with new decoration of the **facade** and substantial transformation, in a Baroque key, of the interior. He added a number of chapels, among which that of the Cybo family, designed by Carlo Fontana. The **interior** of the church is a veritable museum of 13th- through 17th- century art. When he rebuilt the church, Bregno also created the *high altar* and a number of interesting *funeral monuments* in the various chapels; the original altar has now been moved to the sacristy and replaced with the 17th-century altar, where is found the oldest work in the church, the 8th-century panel painting of the *Madonna del Popolo*, once believed to be the work of Saint Luke.

The Cinquecento is represented by the beautiful *frescoes* that decorate the vault of the choir, in which are found two *funeral monuments* by Sansovino that are commonly considered among the artist's finest works. Raphael, after having styled the project for the **Chigi Chapel**, also supplied the cartoon for the *mosaics* that decorate its dome and that dominate from above other extremely valuable works like Sebastiano del Piombo's vivid *Nativity of the Virgin*, Lorenzetto's *Jonah and the Whale*, and *Abacuc and the Angel* by Bernini. The latter artist also left his mark on the decoration throughout the church, with many statues of saints - among which a sublime *Saint Barbara* - designed by him but actually sculpted by Antonio Raggi.

In the **Cerasi Chapel** in the left transept are two masterpieces by Caravaggio: the *Conversion of Saint Paul* and the *Crucifixion of Saint Peter*, painted by the master in 1601-1602.

CHIESA NUOVA

The name Chiesa Nuova (New Church) alludes to the 16th-century renovation of the original building although the church also conserves its ancient denomination of **Santa Maria in Vallicella**, which in turn alludes to a slight depression in the terrain that was later leveled. The 'new' church, like the adjacent oratory by Borromini, is linked to the figure of Saint Philip Neri, the founder of important humanitarian institutions, among which the Confraternita della Santissima Trinità dei Pellegrini e dei Convalescenti, and a zealous apostle of Catholicism. In recognition of Neri's deeds, Pope Gregory XIII granted him the church in 1575; the future saint immediately embarked on reconstruction, entrusting the work first to Matteo da Città di Castello and then to Martino Longhi the Elder. The church was consecrated in 1599 but was completed only early in the following century with the erection of the **facade**, inspired by that of the nearby Church of Gesù, and the decoration of the **interior**, work on which continued on into the 18th century.

The **chapels** also abound in important works of art. The sacristy gives access to the **Rooms of Saint Philip**, on two floors, that were superbly decorated during the 1600s. The rooms contain curios and mementos recalling the saint; in the chapel is an interesting work by Guercino depicting *Saint Philip with an Angel.*

SAN GIOVANNI DEI FIORENTINI

In the early Cinquecento, the Florentine community based in the Ponte district of Rome began to feel the need for a church worthy of representing its wealth and standing. Thus the decision to build a magnificent temple dedicated to Saint John the Baptist, at the end of the Via Giulia. The decisive stimulus to construction of the church was the election of Pope Leo X, of the Florentine Medici dynasty. In 1519, the pope called for plans; the contest was won by Sansovino, who began work on the church but was soon replaced by Antonio da Sangallo the Younger. Work was interrupted in 1527, during the Sack of Rome. In 1559, Michelangelo presented designs for a central-plan church, but they were rejected in favor of Sansovino's original design, on the basis of which Della Porta resumed work in 1583. Maderno completed the **dome** in 1620.

At this point there remained only the **facade**, for which another contest was called by Clement XII, a member of the Florentine Corsini family whose coat-of-arms adorns the tympanum of the center portal. The commission was won by Alessandro Galilei, also the author of the facade of San Giovanni in Laterano, who completed the majestic and austere front decorated with statues and reliefs by Della Valle and other artists. Of note in the **interior** is the presbytery begun by Pietro da Cortona, to whom we owe the gilded coffered ceiling, and completed by Borromini, who is buried here.

SANT'AGNESE IN AGONE

In 1652, as part of the works undertaken for reorganizing Piazza Navona, Innocent X decided to restructure the ancient church of Sant'Agnese, founded by Pope Damasus on the site on which the saint, exposed naked on the pillory but miraculously covered by her own hair, met her death as a martyr. And since the pope's main intention in the work was to give the square a 'face-lift', when he commissioned Carlo and Girolamo Rainaldi to rebuild the church he also required that they invert its original orientation.

After about a year from the start of the work, supervision of the project was turned over to the Ticinese Borromini, who while keeping the Rainaldis' Greek cross plan modified the design of the **facade** to obtain an imaginative concave front that emphasized the slender, soaring **dome**, the interior of which was frescoed by Baciccia and by Ciro Ferri. In 1657, supervision of the work returned into the hands of Carlo Rainaldi; he was succeeded by Baratta and Del Grande, who built the twin **bell towers** to plans by Borromini.

In the **interior**, decorated with gilded stuccowork and precious marbles, are many valuable works of art. The underlying area reveals the ancient history of the site: in the subterranean vaults some traces of Domitian's Stadium are still visible, as are the remains of the original church with 13th-century frescoes and Algardi's last work, a marble bas-relief showing *Saint Agnes Led to Martyrdom*.

SANTA MARIA DELLA PACE

In the 15th century, on the site of today's church, there stood the small medieval oratory of Sant'Andrea de Aquazariis, which obtained considerable notoriety in 1480 when an image of the Virgin began bleeding prodigiously after having been struck by a stone. Sixtus IV thus decided to rebuild the church and to dedicate it to Saint Mary of Virtue, but he died before completion of the work. It continued under Innocent VIII, who gave the church the name it bears today.

Finally, in 1656, Pope Alexander VII Chigi ordered its restructuring. Pietro da Cortona created the two-order **facade**, deftly inserted into the plays of concave and convex surfaces that surround it, and added a singular semicircular **pronaos**, on the architrave of which is an inscription in Latin, reading "To the people, may the mountains bring peace and the hills justice," alluding to the Chigi coat-of-arms, with its six-peaked mountain.

In the striking **interior** is the harmonious **Chigi Chapel**, built to plans by Raphael and frescoed by the artist with the images of four *Sibyls*, and other no-less-interesting chapels including that of the Cesi family designed by Antonio da Sangallo the Younger, who also designed the **dome** of the church, built by Jacopo Ungarino in 1524, and the Pozzetti Chapel, frescoed by Baldassare Peruzzi. To the side of the church is the elegant **cloister** on two superposed orders, built in 1500-1504 for Cardinal Oliviero Carafa, that was Bramante's first commission in Rome.

Sant'Agnese in Agone. The facade with the twin bell towers and the soaring dome; in the foreground, the Fontana dei Quattro Fiumi with the obelisk.

Santa Maria della Pace. The upper portion of the 17th-century facade.

SAN LUIGI DEI FRANCESI

The national church of the French community in Rome was begun in 1518 and completed in 1589, thanks above all to the generosity of Caterina de' Medici, who made available the many family properties in the area. The travertine **facade**, built by Domenico Fontana to plans by Della Porta, opens into a three-aisled **interior** entirely faced in stuccowork and precious marbles in the 18th century by Antoine Derizet and dominated by Natoire's fresco, on the vault, of the *Apotheosis of Saint Louis*, the saint and king to whom the church is dedicated.

But it is in the side chapels, with their frescoes and paintings by the greatest masters of the Roman Seicento, that the most important of the church's artistic treasures are preserved. In 1614, Domenichino decorated the Chapel of Santa Cecilia with some of his most successful frescoes, but it was above all Caravaggio who made this church famous, with the works preserved in the **Contarelli Chapel**. The decoration of the chapel was begun by the Cavalier d'Arpino in 1591 and completed in 1600 by Merisi, who created the three canvases depicting the *Calling* and the *Martyrdom of Saint Matthew* and *Saint Matthew and the Angel*.

Caravaggio's canvas of the Calling of Saint Matthew *in the church of San Luigi dei Francesi, Contarelli Chapel.*

SANT'ANDREA DELLA VALLE

Together with the Gesù and the church of Sant'Ignazio, Sant'Andrea della Valle is an emblem of the Counter-Reformist spirit. It is the most important church of the Theatine monks, that religious order that more coherently than any other incarnated Tridentine orthodoxy. It was in fact a member of the order, Father Grimaldi, who continued the work begun in 1591 by Olivieri and who supervised construction until, in the early 17th century, he was replaced by Maderno, who completed the original structure by raising, in 1622, the enormous **dome** that is second in height only to Saint Peter's. But completion of the **facade** had to wait for Rainaldi, who built it in collaboration with Carlo Fontana to plans by Maderno, inspired by the facade of the Church of Gesù although accentuating the Baroque elements.

The same is true for the **interior**, a huge single nave with a short transept and six communicating side chapels. In the vestibule are two *funeral monuments* transferred here from the Old Saint Peter's Basilica in 1614: both are to Piccolomini popes, Pius II and Pius III, and were created by Andrea Bregno and Sebastiano di Francesco Ferrucci, respectively. The importance of this church nevertheless derives primarily from the many precious works of art that adorn its interior.

SANT'IVO ALLA SAPIENZA

In 1642, the Palazzo della Sapienza, seat of the Roman university, acquired one of the most singular and equally most emblematic creations ever born of the genius of Borromini. He completed the courtyard of the *Studium Urbis*, then terminating in a concave facade, by adding an attic on which he erected the multifoiled lantern of the **dome**, and decorated the intersection with tambours bearing the coat-of-arms of the Chigi family. Over the lantern there rises the tiered 'cap' of the dome, then the *lanternino*, and finally, a ring of travertine torches around the stucco-decorated 'scroll' terminating in a flame, from which a tiara, a globe, and a wrought-iron cross rise.

Sant'Ivo alla Sapienza. The lanternino *designed by Borromini and topped by the stucco-decorated spiral scroll.*

Sant'Andrea della Valle. The 17th-century dome and octagonal tambour with large windows.

The small church of Sant'Eligio degli Orefici, designed by Raphael in the full flower of the Renaissance.

The late-Renaissance facade of the church of San Carlo ai Catinari.

The facade of San Pietro in Montorio, with its double stairway.

SAN CARLO AI CATINARI

This church, commissioned by the Barnabiti fathers in honor of Saint Charles Borromeo shortly after his canonization, owes its name to the many tinsmiths' shops that were situated in the vicinity in the early 17th century, when construction of the church began, and that produced mainly *catini*, or basins and bowls.

Built according to a plan showing the strong influence of late Renaissance architecture, the church, by Rosati - also the author of the tall **dome**, Rome's third highest - was completed in 1638 with the erection of the **facade** by Gian Battista Soria. The works of famous 17th-century artists decorate the interior with superb compositions immortalizing episodes from the life of the dedicatory saint. On the inside facade, Gregorio and Mattia Preti painted two frescoes of *Saint Charles' Crusade against Heresy* and *Saint Charles Giving Alms*, and in the facing vault of the apse Lanfranco depicted *Saint Charles in Glory*; the **choir** was decorated by Guido Reni with a beautiful *Praying Saint Charles*, and finally, on the high altar, the work of Martino Longhi the Younger, is Pietro da Cortona's depiction of *Saint Charles leading a procession in Milan to ward off the plague.*

Domenichino painted the four *Cardinal Virtues* in the pendentives of the dome in about 1630, and toward the end of the century Antonio Gherardi, who had previously worked on the decoration of Santa Maria in Trivio, completed the theatrical ornamentation of the Chapel of Saint Cecilia with imaginative, elaborate plays of color and perspective.

SANT'ELIGIO DEGLI OREFICI

This small jewel of Roman Renaissance architecture, the headquarters of the Confraternity of Goldsmiths, is one of the rare surviving works by Raphael in the guise of architect. Although it clearly shows the influence of Bramante, the design of the building is Raphael's alone, and the artist from Urbino personally supervised the start of its construction in 1516. The work was brought to completion by Baldassare Peruzzi, who took over as site manager at Raphael's death in 1520. The **facade** of the small Greek-cross church, with its graciously airy, small hemispherical **dome**, was seriously damaged in the following century and was rebuilt by Flaminio Ponzio, who created a simple, well-proportioned frontage in perfect keeping with Raphael's original plan.

The same absolute economy of form also dominates in the **interior**, which Raphael probably expected to decorate himself. Its surprisingly elegant simplicity lends harmonizes well with the works by Romanelli and Taddeo Zuccari that adorn the walls.

SAN PIETRO IN MONTORIO AND BRAMANTE'S TEMPIETTO

The pontificate of Sixtus IV, who promoted many urban and public works at the foot of the Janiculum hill and in the adjacent Trastevere area, was sealed, so to speak, with the construction of a church between 1481 and 1500 by Ferdinand II of Aragon. The **church** and **convent** of San Pietro in Montorio rose on the spot where an ancient and unfounded tradition held that the first pope of the Church was martyred (in

reality Saint Peter was crucified in the Stadium of Nero, next to San Pietro in Vaticano).

The complex, built on the site of an earlier 9th-century church, was designed by Baccio Pontelli in the most complete respect of Renaissance architectural dictates. It nevertheless displays the enduring Gothic influence, traceable in the rose window of the simple **facade** of the church. The facade, to which the staircase was added in the 1600s, is attributed to the school of Andrea Bregno.

The **interior**, with its single nave with cross and domical vaults, has many side chapels. The first chapel to the right of the entrance holds an intense *Flagellation of Christ*, done in 1518 by Sebastiano del Piombo from a probable design of Michelangelo, while the fourth chapel on the same side contains the *Conversion of St. Paul* by Vasari, whose self-portrait is the man dressed in black on the left side. Until 1809 the apse contained the *Transfiguration* by Raphael, since moved to the Vatican Galleries and substituted by a copy of the *Crucifixion of St. Peter* by Guido Reni, whose original is also in the Vatican. The works carried out during the Baroque period are best and most completely represented by the fine **Raymondi Chapel** of Gian Lorenzo Bernini.

But the jewel of San Pietro in Montorio is the **Tempietto of Bramante**, built by the architect between 1508 and 1512 in the first cloister of the convent (rebuilt in the early 16th century) above the hole supposedly made by the cross of St. Peter. Sacred tradition and the ideals of classical antiquity induced Bramante to choose a circular plan, the quintessence of architecture and idealized space typical of the Renaissance. The structure is articulated by Etruscan columns and a hemispheric cupola; a surrounding circular courtyard was designed by Bramante to grace the small temple, but it was never executed. The interior encloses two overlapping spaces: the upper area, redesigned during the Baroque period and containing a 16th-century *statue of St. Peter* by the Lombard school; and below, the *crypt* - reached by a double ramp of stairs by Bernini - with the hole made by the cross on which the saint was erroneously said to have died.

The Tempietto of Bramante, a pure expression of the artistic conceptions of the Renaissance.

The interior of Santa Maria sopra Minerva.

SANTA MARIA SOPRA MINERVA

The only church in Rome to have conserved its original Gothic floor-plan, Santa Maria sopra Minerva rose in the 13th century on what at the time were believed to be the ruins of the ancient Temple of Minerva Chalcidicea (actually buried under the nearby church of Santa Marta). Despite the heavy 19th-century restoration work which partially altered its forms, the building, with its three beautiful portals that during the Renaissance were added to the plain **facade**, is stylistically attributable to architects of Tuscan origin or training.

But this church is also linked to Tuscany for other reasons. It is the home of the **Carafa Chapel**, a true gem of 15th-century art. Giuliano da Maiano was the author, with Mino da Fiesole (whose is also the *Tomb of Francesco Tornabuoni* near the entrance) and Verrocchio, of the splendid arch over the entrance, while Filippino Lippi frescoed the walls with the *Triumph of Saint Thomas* and the *Miracles of the Crucifixion* and painted the *Annunciation* over the altar. Tuscany is also recalled by the two *funeral monuments* created by Antonio da Sangallo the Younger in memory of the two Florentine popes, Leo X and Clement VII (in the choir, which was specially altered to host them in 1536); and by the *sarcophagus* containing the relics of Saint Catherine of Siena under the high altar. The small oratory dedicated to the saint and the chamber in which she died are in the **sacristy**, which is decorated with 15th-century frescoes. Another work by another great Tuscan artist is the *tombstone of Fra' Beato Angelico,* sculpted by Isaia da Pisa in 1455; the *Risen Christ* (1520) against the left pilaster of the presbytery is attributed to Michelangelo.

Church of Gesù. The altar of Saint Ignatius and a detail of the facade.

CHURCH OF GESU'

Emblem of the spirit of the Counter-Reform, the Gesù unites formal rigor, inspired by that orthodoxy confirmed by the Council of Trent, with a taste for the pomp and the spatial dramatization typical of the Baroque. Following the building of the church, which began in 1568, the latter style supplied a worthy decorative complement to the straightforward and weighty structure of the church itself, designed by Ignatius Loyola.

Twenty or so years earlier, the founder of the Society of Jesus had received the small church of Santa Maria della Strada (or 'degli Astalli') from Pope Paul III. He decided to enlarge it with financing provided by Cardinal Alessandro Farnese: Vignola drew up the plans for the church itself; the massive yet anything but ungracious travertine **facade** is instead the work of Giacomo Della Porta. For the **interior**, in line with the new liturgical needs dictated by the Council of Trent, Vignola designed a single nave, with side chapels, intersected by a transept of equal width and with a hemispherical dome, which was later adorned with frescoes by Baciccia. In 1679, the same artist also decorated the **vault** of the nave with the spectacular *Triumph of the Holy Name of Jesus*, an admirable example of the illusionistic perspective painting typical of the Baroque that is accentuated by the dilation of the paintwork beyond Raggi's gilded stucco cornice to invade the vault and even the structural ribbing of the church. The side chapels, although simple, contain valuable works; the showpiece is the Chapel of Saint Ignatius, a work by the Je-

suit Father Andrea Pozzo, in which the body of the saint is entombed. This grandiose late 17th-century Baroque work culminates in the **Altar of Saint Ignatius**, which is set off by a profluvium of decoration that ranges from the gilded bronze of the reliefs showing *Scenes from the Life of Saint Ignatius* to the lapis lazuli that constellate the columns and the niche that shelters the silver-sheathed *statue of the saint*, a copy of the original by Pierre Legros. Alongside the church stands the **Casa Professa**, in 1543 the seat of the Society of Jesus and the site of Saint Ignatius Loyola's death in 1586.

SANT'IGNAZIO DI LOYOLA

A magniloguent monument to Counter-Reformist orthodoxy, this church, dedicated to the founder of the Society of Jesus, sanctified by Pope Gregory XV four years prior to the construction of the church (1626), echoes the at once simple and spectacular forms of the nearby Church of Gesù.

By order of the pope who had canonized Saint Ignatius, this church replaced the earlier Santissima Annunziata, which had become too small for the needs of the well-attended Collegio Romano where the Jesuit friars were trained. One of their number, Father Orazio Grassi, designed the three-aisled structure in which the center nave nevertheless greatly preponderates; the **vault** of the nave was frescoed by another Jesuit, Father Andrea Pozzo, with the *Glory of Saint Ignatius*, an authentic masterpiece of illusionistic prospective composition.

San Carlino alle Quattro Fontane. A detail of the curved facade and the interior of the elliptical dome with the lacunars forming various patterns, including the crosses symbolizing the Order of the Trinitarians who commissioned Borromini to build the church.

Right, Sant'Andrea al Quirinale. The high altar framed by four Corinthian columns supporting the pediment with the statue of Saint Andrew, and the splendid, richly gilded, gored and coffered ceiling of the elliptical dome.

SANT'ANDREA AL QUIRINALE

A masterpiece by Gian Lorenzo Bernini, Sant'Andrea al Quirinale was commissioned of the great master in 1658
by Pope Alexander VII with the support
of Prince Camillo Pamphili, to replace
an earlier 16th-century church used by
the adjacent Jesuit Noviciate, today
used as offices.
Underlying the peculiar architectural
syntax of Bernini's building are the ellipse and the semicircle. The interior
space is in fact elliptical, as is the dome
and the lantern topping it; the *pro-
thyrum*, the entrance staircase, and the
window that opens in the quadrangular
facade are instead all semicircular.
The **interior** was later decorated, to
plans by Bernini, by Antonio Raggi,
who populated the spaces above the
great arched windows, the gilded coffered cupola, and the lantern with figures of *putti* and cherubim arranged in
such a manner as to lend theatrical em-
phasis to the central scene. Bor-
gognone's excellent *Martyrdom of
Saint Andrew* on the high altar is preceded by a columned aedicula with
the *Glory of Saint Andrew* by Raggi.

SAN CARLINO ALLE QUATTRO FONTANE

Near the Quattro Fontane crossroads, this small church, the dimensions of which
are more or less equivalent to those of one of the four pylons that support the
dome of Saint Peter's, is one of the jewels of Roman Baroque architecture. Borromini was commissioned to build it and the adjacent convent by the Spanish Trinitarians, who had chosen the site as their seat in the early 1600s; the church was
begun in 1638 and terminated, as regards its essential structures, in 1641.
The **facade** took a while longer. It is concave at the sides and convex at the center;
its wealth of moldings, columns, niches, and statues create a lively and imaginative architectural score.
The curvilinear theme of the exterior of the church is taken up again in the **interi-
or**, but here Borromini also accentuated the vertical development of the structure,
where the **elliptical dome** - decorated according to an intricate scheme of cruci-
form coffering, the hexagonal and octagonal lacunars becoming smaller and
smaller as they approach the lantern - exalts the perspective and suggests a space
larger than that actually available. The lower church repeats the motifs and forms
of the upper church, as does the adjoining **cloister**, with its harmonious and elegant proportions.
In creating this complex masterpiece, Borromini took attention to detail to an ex-
treme: he even designed the confessionals and the wrought-iron rail of the well at
the center of the cloister.

THE SPANISH STEPS AND THE CHURCH OF TRINITÀ DEI MONTI

In 1728, Montesquieu, then traveling in Italy, saw the Spanish Steps, completed only several years earlier. Surprisingly, his opinion was negative. "The Scalinata di Trinità dei Monti," he wrote, "is in bad taste. There is no architecture of any kind, and it can barely be seen, except for the first ramp. They should have made it a fine work and put up some columns. Moreover, the work was done so poorly that part of it has collapsed."

Although the historical fact about the partial collapse is true, caused by a movement of the earth beneath the hill, the opinion of the French philosopher on the harmonious stairway is not widely shared. Ordered by Pope Innocent XIII and initiated by the architect Francesco De Sanctis in 1723, the Spanish Steps impress the thousands of visitors who come every day to enjoy the monument, now one of the symbols of Rome and of all of Italy.

The ascent to the church of Trinità dei Monti, which was once reached by tree-lined paths, is now made on the sinuous stairs formed by a succession of twelve ramps, which split apart and reconnect in a play of perspectives. The focal points throughout remain the church itself and the **Sallustian Obelisk**, once in the *Horti Sallustiani* and placed here by Antinori in 1789, under Pius VI. The decorations of the stairs include the heraldic eagle of the Conti family, to which Innocent XIII belonged, and the French lily, since the **church of Trinità dei Monti** was French. The church and the adjoining convents were built by King Louis XII of France in 1502 and consecrated some 80 years later by Sixtus V in occasion of the opening of the Strada Felice, which passed in front of the church. Restored in the 1800s, the church now has a universally known **facade,** with two characteristic twin belltowers by Maderno, perhaps from a design of Giacomo Della Porta. The **interior**, with a rich collection of art and impressive architecture, has numerous side chapels adorned with paintings by Perin del Vaga, the Zuccari brothers and especially Daniele da Volterra, with his famous and intense *Deposition*.

SANT'ANDREA DELLE FRATTE

In the 12th century, this church was so far beyond the inhabited area that it received the name Sant'Andrea de Hortis, meaning 'of the gardens'. Later the name was changed to the more prosaic '*de Fractis*' and then 'delle Fratte' (thickets), the name it has kept. Originally belonging to the Scots and donated by Sixtus V to the Minim friars of San Francesco di Paola, it was entirely rebuilt by Gaspare Guerra for the marquis De Bufalo in the early 1600s and completed by Borromini in the middle of the same century.

It was Borromini who designed the semi-elliptical apse, the unfinished drum of the cupola, and the original **campanile**, which can admired in all of its bold architectural conception from Via Capo le Case. The tower is a square structure on several levels, surmounted by a fanciful crowning of hermae in the shape of cherubs holding the *cross of St. Andrew* and the *buffalo*, the heraldic symbol of the commissioning family. It is all topped by a metal crown like that of Sant'Ivo alla Sapienza.

The **interior**, with a single nave and barrel vaults, has among its works two pieces by another genius of Roman Baroque, who was said to be the implacable adversary of Borromini. The two beautiful **angels** are in fact by Bernini, the *Angel with the Crown of Thorns* and the *Angel with a Scroll*. Sculpted by the master between 1668 and 1669 to decorate Ponte Sant'Angelo, they were brought here to save them from the elements. One of the side chapels provides

access to the **cloister** of the adjoining convent of the Minim, where lunettes with frescoes depicting the *Story of San Francesco di Paola* can be admired.

Trinità dei Monti.
The plaque giving the history of the famous Spanish Steps.

A view of the Sallustian Obelisk.

Above, right, the inscription on the facade of the Palazzo di Propaganda Fide.

Left, the original campanile of Sant'Andrea delle Fratte.

Trinità dei Monti. The church, with its facade and the characteristic twin belltowers, at the top of the Spanish Steps.

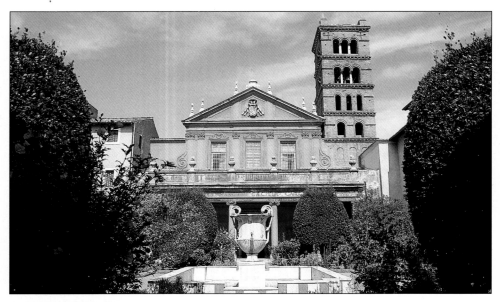

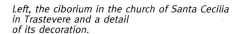

Santa Cecilia in Trastevere. The facade on the courtyard, with its garden, and the fine Romanesque bell tower.

Left, the ciborium in the church of Santa Cecilia in Trastevere and a detail of its decoration.

SANTA CECILIA IN TRASTEVERE

This basilica in Trastevere is dedicated to the young martyr Cecilia, who according to tradition lived here with her husband Valerian, sainted as well. Despite its having been remodeled many times over the centuries, the complex has preserved all its ancient charm with its series of courtyards and other structures in the shade of a superb Romanesque **bell tower** crowned by unmistakable pinnacles, its still-inhabited enclosed convent, with its marvelous cloister, and the innumerable masterpieces of art preserved within its walls.

The church was built on the site of the *titulus Caeciliae* before Pope Paschal I's reign in the fifth century, and was in large part rebuilt in about 1110. Other remodeling followed; not the least important was the work that in the 19th century 'imprisoned' the ancient columns of the nave, which threatened to crumble, in pillars.

In the 1700s, Ferdinando Fuga created the theatrical **entrance** that leads to a large garden **courtyard** with at its center a sizeable marble basin used in Roman times as a fountain. The courtyard is overlooked, as well as by the bell tower, by the Baroque facade of the church, which is preceded by a charming **portico** decorated with an elegant mosaic frieze dating to the 12th century. Under the arches, alongside numerous medieval finds, is the *monument to Cardinal Sfondrati*, designed by Girolamo Rainaldi (or by Stefano Maderno), commemorating the prelate who engineered the finding of the body of Saint Cecilia. The interior, preceded by an **atrium** with the *monument to Cardinal Forteguerri* by Mino da Fiesole, is in 18th-century style with a wide **nave**, the ceiling of which was frescoed by Conca with the *Apotheosis of Saint Cecilia*.

Off the aisles, which are embellished with valuable paintings including Guido Reni's *Saint Valerian and Saint Cecilia*, there open a number of interesting chapels. The name of the harmonious *Calidario Chapel*, in late Renaissance style with stuccowork decoration and paintings of scenes from the life of the martyr, recalls the room that in Roman times was used for steam bathing and in which, as tradition narrates, Cecilia's persecutors left her for three days in an attempt to suffocate her - but from which she escaped unscathed. The 15th-century *Ponziani Chapel* is decorated with beautiful coeval frescoes and a Cosmati-work altar facing; the *Reliquary Chapel* was designed by Luigi Vanvitelli, also the author of the altarpiece and the fresco in the vault.

But the portion of the basilica that more than any other preserves works of intense artistic inspiration is the **apse** with its facing **presbytery**. Here, as though projected

Interior of Santa Cecilia in Trastevere.
Details of the Last Judgment by Pietro
Cavallini (13th cent.) and of the portraits
of Saints Paschal, Cecilia, and Paul, in
the Byzantine mosaic in the
apse (9th cent.)

against the luminous, 9th-century Byzantine mosaics of the vault of the apse, portraying the *Blessing Christ with Saints Paul, Cecilia, Paschal I* (shown with a square halo because he was still alive when the work was created), *Peter, Valerian, and Agatha* and the allegory of the *Mystical Lamb*, there dominates Arnolfo di Cambio's **altar canopy**: created in 1293, this elegant masterpiece by the Tuscan artist is like an embroidery in marble constellated with the gracious figures of angels, saints, prophets, and the evangelists.

The ciborium in turn contains another outstanding sculpture: the **statue of Saint Cecilia** sculpted by Stefano Maderno, who used as his model the body of the young martyr, found intact during the excavations in the Catacombs of San Callisto on the Via Appia ordered in 1599 by Cardinal Sfondrati. The saint is portrayed as she lay, with her face turned aside and her hands showing the one three and the other one finger to symbolize the dogma of the Trinity she would not abandon even at the moment of her death.

The left aisle leads to the 13th-century cloister, which opens into the **nuns' choir** room with its fine **Last Judgment** by Pietro Cavallini, a medieval fresco more or less coeval with Arnolfo di Cambio's canopy. Although it has reached us in a fragmentary state, it is still an intensely dramatic work showing *Christ* between the beseeching *Virgin* and *Saint John the Baptist*; the group is surrounded by the *Apostles* and around the whole is a *Choir of Angels* and fragments of celestial and infernal visions with the ranks of the blessed and the reprobates.

SANTA MARIA DELL'ORTO

This church, specially built by an unknown architect of Bramante's circle to house a *Virgin with Child* detached from the wall of a garden (hence the name of the church), was begun in 1495 and completed halfway through the following century by Guidetto Guidetti. Its construction was financed by the contributions of many Roman craftsmen's congregations, among which the quaint and now-defunct 'Universities' of the grocers, the poulterers, and the vermicelli-makers, as is testified in the adjacent **oratory**.

Although the 16th-century facade begun by Vignola and completed by Francesco da Volterra is still intact, the Renaissance **interior** is mostly masked by the vivacious Baroque decoration that frames Zuccari's precious 16th-century paintings in the apse and Baglione's frescoes on the walls of the presbytery and in some of the side chapels.

The Renaissance facade of the church of
Santa Maria dell'Orto.

SANTA MARIA IN TRASTEVERE

Traditionally, this church is considered the first to have been opened for worship in Rome and in any case the first to be dedicated to the Virgin Mary. The *titulus Calisti* was founded in the third century by Pope Calixtus I and dedicated to him after he was sainted. It rose on the site on which, according to the chronicles of the times, the earth erupted oil in 38 BC, an event later construed as a miraculous annunciation of the birth of Christ. The *Fons Olei* (Fount of Oil) is still marked by a plaque set near the presbytery of the church.

On the site, Pope Julius I had a basilica-like structure built; the final form is, however, the result of later alterations dating to the pontificate of Innocent II, who between 1130 and 1143 had the building restructured using materials taken from the Baths of Caracalla; nevertheless, neither the original basilica plan nor the placement of the twenty-two ancient granite columns that separate the aisles were modified.

In 1702, Clement XI charged Carlo Fontana with rebuilding the **portico**, which, with its rich collection of epigraphs, marbles, and Roman and Christian reliefs, stands against the beautiful **facade** with its curious horizontal concave molding surmounted by a tympanum and a 13th-century *mosaic* band (perhaps retouched by Pietro Cavallini) portraying the *Virgin Enthroned with Two Donors* and two *Processions of Women*. Alongside rises the massive Romanesque **bell tower**, culminating in a 17th-century aedicula.

At the rear of the **nave**, with its elaborate coffered *wooden ceiling* designed by Domenichino (who also painted the center canvas of the *Assumption of the Virgin*), is the beautiful **apse** decorated with elegant gold-ground *mosaics* from two different eras. Those of the triumphal arch and the vault are from the 1100s; those of the lower register, divided into panels, date to the end of the following century. The first series, created following the death of Innocent II in 1143, portrays on the arch the *Symbols of the Evangelists* and the *Prophets Jeremiah and Isaiah* and in the half-dome of the apse *Christ Crowing the Virgin* with to the left and right a series of figures of saints and popes involved in the various phases of construction of the church. Immediately below, the strip depicting the *Mystical Lamb* surrounded by twelve sheep, symbols of the Apostles, concludes the older series of mosaics. The panels depicting *Scenes from the Life of the Virgin* were instead created in 1291 by Pietro Cavallini for Cardinal Bertoldo Stefaneschi, who is shown as a donor in the medallion of the *Virgin and Child with Saints Peter and Paul*.

The additions in modern times were many: the *Altemps Chapel*, built for Cardinal Marco Sittico Altemps by Martino Longhi the Elder in 1585, contains the Byzantine-style encaustic of the *Madonna della Clemenza*; the *Avila Chapel* dates to the following century and was designed by Antonio

Santa Maria in Trastevere. Above, the upper portion of the facade and the Romanesque-style bell tower.

Center, the interior with the vault of the apse and the triumphal arch, both decorated with mosaics, with at the center the marble ciborium.

Below, a detail of the mosaic on the facade, with the Virgin Enthroned *(13th cent.).*

Interior of Santa Maria in Trastevere. Twelfth-century bishop's throne.

Gherardi, who employed his genius in creating exuberant trompe-l'oiel effects above all in the imaginative small dome that appears to be supported by four flying angels; the tiny *Baptistery Chapel*, by Filippo Raguzzini, is instead a true masterpiece of the rococo, dated 1741.

SAN CRISOGONO

This third largest of the medieval basilicas in Trastevere was built on the 5th-century *titulus Chrysogoni* in 1123-1129 by order of Cardinal Giovanni da Crema, who had the original basilica filled in. Portions of the structure can still be seen below today's church, together with some of the frescoes that decorated its walls and apse.

Despite the transformation of the structure in the 17th century, the 12th-century plan suffered no major modifications. In 1620-1626, Giovanni Battista Soria directed the renovation of the building promoted by Cardinal Scipione Borghese.

On the exterior, he rebuilt the **portico**, using the same granite columns used in the Middle Ages, but he left substantially intact the mighty **bell tower**, built in 1124, adding only the spire.

Soria's hand in the interior was also rather restrained. He retained the 13th-century medieval basilica plan, with its three aisles divided by twenty-two ancient granite columns, its beautiful Cosmatesque floor, and the **apse**, the vault of which is still refulgent with the splendid mosaic, by Pietro Cavallini's school, of the *Virgin and Child with Saint Crysogonus and Saint James*.

Bernini is instead the author of the **Chapel of the Holy Sacrament** at the end of the right aisle, and his pupils of the sculptures decorating it.

SAN FRANCESCO A RIPA

Once the property, together with the adjoining 10th-century **monastery**, of the Benedictines who various times offered hospitality to Saint Francis, the church was acquired in 1229 by the Friars Minor, who also occupied the monastery and in the 1250s promoted various renovation actions.

Saint Francis' presence is attested to by a copy (the original is in the Pinacoteca Vaticana) of the *effigy of the saint*, attributed to Fra' Margaritone d'Arezzo, in the Chapel of Relics.

In the simple three-aisled church, rebuilt by Mattia De Rossi in the late 1600s, the Paluzzi Albertoni Chapel is home to a masterpiece of Baroque sculpture, the statue of **Blessed Ludovica Albertoni**, a powerful late work by Bernini that in certain ways is superior to his *Saint Theresa* in Santa Maria della Vittoria.

Interior of Santa Maria in Trastevere. The apse mosaic of the Presentation in the Temple *from the series* Scenes from the Life of the Virgin *(13th cent.).*

San Crisogono. The facade with the 17th-century portico and the massive Romanesque bell tower.

Interior of San Francesco a Ripa. The death of the Blessed Ludovica Albertoni as portrayed by Bernini in a late work (1675).

SANTI GIOVANNI E PAOLO

The brief return by the emperor Julian the Apostate to the ancient pagan religion and to the persecution of Christians culminated in 362 with the murder of the two officials of the imperial guard, Giovanni (John) and Paolo (Paul), to whom the church is dedicated. It was built in 398, by the Roman senator and saint Pammachius and his father Bizante, on the site of the martyrs' torture and death, but was soon thereafter damaged during the 5th-century barbarian incursions. After being sacked for the nth time in 1084 by the Normans, Pope Paschal II had the church restored at the same time that the adjoining convent and the beautiful **bell tower** were being built. The tower was completed in the 12th century together with the **portico** that replaced the original narthex.

After renovations in the 1700s and 1800s, mid-20th century restoration revealed what remained of the early structures of the church: for instance, the lovely marble *five-lighted windows* of the 4th-century facade and the beautiful 13th-century *portal* with its Cosmati-work inlays and an eagle sculpted in the architrave.

The interior, with a *plaque* halfway along the nave marking the site of the martyrdom of John and Paul, persists in its 18th-century guise. Traces of the past are instead clearly visible in the intricate labyrinth of the **foundations**, which incorporate the remains of five buildings raised between the 1st and the 4th centuries for a total of about 20 rooms.

SANTA MARIA IN DOMNICA

The first church, raised in the 7th century on the remains of one of the barracks of the ancient Celian military complex, was rebuilt a couple of centuries later under Pope Paschal I. It then remained unaltered until 1513, when Cardinal Giovanni de' Medici, the future Pope Leo X, had it restored by Sansovino, who is undoubtedly the author of the elegant five-arch **portico**; tradition ascribes its design to Raphael. Although documentation proving authorship does not exist, the Raphaelesque matrix is clearly visible in both this and much of the other work conducted in the 1500s.

SANTO STEFANO ROTONDO

As the name itself suggests, this is one of Rome's three early-Christian circular-plan structures (together with the Baptistery of San Giovanni in Laterano and the church of Santa Costanza), all built during the first two centuries of Christendom and directly derived from analogous Roman constructions, typically those of the city's bath complexes. The building, completed in the 5th century and consecrated by Pope Simplicius, was originally composed of three concentric aisles divided by columns and intersected by the arms of a Greek cross structure. The early church began to undergo changes under Pope Innocent II (1300s) when a **portico** with columns taken from ancient monuments was added; a couple of centuries later, a transversal **colonnade** was built.

Santi Giovanni e Paolo. The front portico.

Santa Maria in Domnica. The apse mosaic of the Virgin and Child.

The 34 columns of the exterior ambulacrum were encased in the perimeter wall, along which, in the late 1500s, Pomarancio and Tempesta painted the *Martyrology*: thirty-four dramatic frescoes that show, with what is often explicit bluntness, the tortures to which the same number of saints were subjected.
The central portion of the church, separated from the exterior ambulacrum by twenty-two marble columns with Corinthian capitals, has a high **drum** in which a series of cambered windows, some of which with two lights, were opened during the 15th-century restorations.

SAN GREGORIO MAGNO AND THE THREE ORATORIES

Today's complex structure rises on the site of the monastery of Saint Andrew the Apostle founded by Saint Gregory the Great in 575. The **facade** by Giovanni Battista Soria, on the model of that of San Luigi dei Francesi, stands at the summit of a wide staircase. In the large courtyard are three oratories, or chapels, that were renovated in the early 17th century by Cardinal Baronio. That of **Sant'Andrea**, probably the original church founded by Saint Gregory, conserves two famous frescoes: the *Flagellation of Saint Andrew* by Domenichino and *Saint Andrew Led to Martyrdom* by Guido Reni. The oratory of **Santa Barbara**, or Oratory of the Triclinium, is also part of the original construction and owes its name to the ancient stone table on which it is said Saint Gregory offered food to twelve poor people who were later joined by a shining angel. The last oratory, dedicated to Saint Gregory's mother **Santa Silvia**, was built by Baronio; in the apse is Guido Reni's *Concert of Angels*.

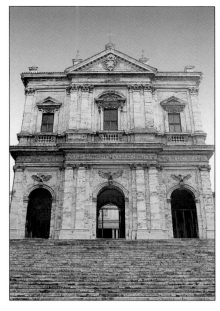

The facade of San Gregorio Magno.

SAN SISTO VECCHIO

This medieval church was totally rebuilt in the 1700s by Raguzzini, who left only the soaring 12th-century **bell tower** intact. The church was granted in 1219 to Saint Dominic, who established his first monastery here; off the cloister, on what is traditionally considered the site of the saint's cell, is the **chapel** dedicated to him. In the interior of the church, among the flights of Raguzzini's architectural fancy, are traces of the building's medieval past in the 14th-century cycle of *frescoes* in the apse.

Santo Stefano Rotondo.
The circular-plan interior.

Interior of Santa Maria in Aracoeli. Above, the tomb of Cardinal Matteo d'Acquasparta and the fresco of the Virgin Enthroned with Two Saints above it.

Sant'Agnese fuori le Mura. Apse mosaic.

Santa Costanza. Plant and flower motifs in the decoration.

Right, the propylaea of the Porticus of Octavia.

SANTA MARIA IN ARACOELI

The date of construction of this church, a true jewel of medieval architecture, is uncertain: it is variously dated to the time of Constantine and to that of Gregory the Great. The most probable hypothesis, however, is that by which it was built in the 8th century for the Greek monks. The good friars were supplanted first by the Benedictines and later by the Franciscans, who in the 13th century enlarged and restructured the building to plans probably by Arnolfo di Cambio. This phase of work was concluded with the construction of the steep **staircase** inaugurated in 1348, but in the centuries that followed further remodeling partially altered the pre-existing medieval building.

The suggestive **interior** is divided into a nave and two aisles by columns from various monuments of ancient Rome, and is home to works of great artistic importance. The Bufalini Chapel preserves late 15th-century frescoes by Pinturicchio of *Stories from the Life of Saint Bernardino*, considered one of the artist's masterpieces, but the remaining chapels, the transepts and the aisles are certainly no less noteworthy. For example, in the Savelli Chapel in the right transept is the beautiful *tomb of Luca Savelli*, attributed to Arnolfo di Cambio, which integrates a finely-decorated Roman sarcophagus with a lovely 14th-century marble structure with mosaic inlays.

Another interesting funerary monument is the Cosmatesque *tomb of Cardinal Matteo d'Acquasparta*, in the left transept, set in a Gothic aedicula decorated with a fresco attributed to Cavallini.

SANT'AGNESE FUORI LE MURA

This building, dating from the period of Constantine, was rebuilt in the 7th century in the Byzantine style, as seen in the *matroneum* (gallery reserved for women in early Christian churches) and the apsidal *mosaics* on a gold background depicting *Saint Agnes between Popes Symmachus and Honorius I*, with the latter pope holding a model of the basilica. The saint is instead represented with the symbols of martyrdom, the sword and flame, and with a phoenix on her robe, symbol of immortality. Inside of the church is the entrance to the **Catacombs of St. Agnes**, containing the body of the saint, martyred during the persecutions of Diocletian.

SANTA COSTANZA

An undisputed jewel of early Christian architecture, the church was built in the 4th century as a mausoleum for the daughters of Constantine, Costantia and Helena. Along with Santo Stefano Rotondo and the Baptistery of San Giovanni in Laterano, Santa Costanza is the city's oldest Christian building on a circular plan.

With its original structure still mostly intact, the church opens around a circular central space punctuated by paired marble columns that set off the annular nave, or **ambulatory**. The barrel vaults are decorated with 4th-century *mosaics* in which plant, geometric, and figurative motifs alternate with figures of animals and cupids still inspired by pagan designs. Christian motifs are instead found in the mosaics of the two side **niches**, showing *Christ Giving the Keys to St. Peter* and *Christ Delivering the Gospel*.

SANT'ANGELO IN PESCHERIA

The church of **Sant'Angelo in Pescheria**, of which the Porticus acts as pronaos, was the object of extensive early Renaissance remodeling in the 1400s, when it was given the pillars separating the nave from the two aisles and the trussed wooden ceiling. The second chapel on the left contains a fresco, attributed to Benozzo Gozzoli, of the *Virgin with the Child and Angels*.

THE MONUMENTS OF ROME

COLOSSEUM

CIRCUS MAXIMUS

PALAZZO SENATORIO

MAUSOLEUM OF AUGUSTUS

COLUMN OF MARCUS AURELIUS

CASTEL SANT'ANGELO

FONTANA DI TREVI

TEMPLE OF VESTA

ARA PACIS AUGUSTAE

The Colosseum and its interior, made up of a cavea and an arena. The different sectors of seats in the cavea were assigned from lower to higher by decreasing social standing, the tiers nearest the arena being reserved for the senators.
The center of the arena was originally covered by wooden planks; the subterranean chambers, on three concentric passageways with openings connecting the different sectors, were used for storing material connected with the spectacles, from wild beasts in cages to the gladiators' weapons.

THE COLOSSEUM

Following the fire of 64 AD that destroyed a goodly part of the city, Nero decided to build his grandiose *Domus Aurea* on the Oppian hill. It was linked to the facing Palatine hill by a cryptoporticus, part of which is still standing. The depression between the two heights was the site of gardens and a man-made lake, not far from which, to mark the entrance to the palace, there stood a colossal gilded bronze statue of the emperor as Sun God. In 72 AD, Vespasian ordered that the lake be drained in order to build an amphitheater, construction of which continued under Titus until the year 79. These two emperors, both of the Flavian dynasty, were responsible for the first name given the building, which was known in antiquity as the **Amphiteatrum Flavium**.
The name Colosseum dates instead to the Middle Ages and refers to the colossal statue of Nero that Hadrian had moved near the celebrated monument. The amphitheater was inau-

gurated in 80 AD with spectacles and games that lasted, according to sources of the time, one hundred days, during which thousands of wild animals and many gladiators were killed in combat. When, under Domitian, the top tier was completed with the construction of an attic and the supports to which the *velarium* (an immense tent that shielded the spectators from the sun), the structure had a capacity of 50,000 spectators, who sat in the *cavea*, an area separated from the enormous elliptical arena, 86 meters by 54, by a podium protected by a balustrade. It was here that important personages were seated, while a special box was reserved for the emperor and the Vestals. The cavea, built entirely of marble, was subdivided into orders and sectors; the seats were occupied from lower to higher in accordance with social standing, the highest order of seats being 'reserved' for the plebs. The area underlying the arena was instead riddled with galleries where the animals used in the spectacles were stabled and where the scenic devices were stored; at the ends of the galleries were elevators for transporting persons and things to the surface.
The travertine exterior facade of the amphitheater had three superposed series of arches delimited by semicolumns in the three classical styles, Doric, Ionic, and Corinthian, and an attic decorated with pilaster strips, for an overall height of about 50 meters.
During the Middle Ages, earthquakes brought down certain

parts of the structure; the remains were for a time transformed into fortifications controlled by the Frangipane family. The amphitheater later became an immense 'quarry' for building materials used in churches and palaces, until in 1744 Pope Benedict XIV consecrated the Colosseum to the martyrs of the Faith and issued an edict banning any further demolition. Later restoration campaigns, the first of which began in 1805, have targeted recovering the original structure.

THE ARCH OF CONSTANTINE

Built in 315 by the 'Senate and the People of Rome' in celebration of Constantine's victory over Maxentius in 312 in the battle of the Milvian Bridge, fought and won by the emperor by 'divine inspiration', as the dedicatory inscription on the attic tells us, this arch may be said to be the last great monument of pagan antiquity. But it is also the ideal symbol of the beginning of the Christian era, since it was following the battle that Constantine, with the Edict of Milan of 313, acknowledged the right of Roman citizens to practice the Christian religion and the authority of the Bishop of Rome.

The monumental structure, with its *three openings*, is about 20 meters high and is decorated with statues and reliefs that were in part created for the occasion and in part recovered from earlier buildings and analogous monuments.

For example, the panels on the *attic* are from the Arch of Marcus Aurelius and show this emperor's triumph in 174; the interior of the center arch is decorated with two reliefs originally in the Basilica Ulpia in Trajan's Forum. This forum was also the original home of the statues of Dacian prisoners on the attic above the columns, which in turn were recovered from the Domitian's Arch. The tondi showing episodes of different types - among which hunting scenes - are from Hadrian's Arch, but the reliefs in the side strip panels, depicting the story of the emperor's triumph over Maxentius, were created specially for the arch.

Top, the Colosseum.

Right: The Arch of Constantine (top) was modeled on the Arch of Septimius Severus (center). The Arch of Titus (bottom) was built in his honor by his successor Domitian in memory of the Jewish campaign of 70 AD.

The Roman Forum, with a portion of the Via Sacra, the Temple of Antoninus and Faustina on the left, and the Temple of Vesta on the right; in the background, Santa Francesca Romana and the Colosseum.

The remains of the House of the Vestals.

The distinctively circular form of the Temple of Vesta in an aerial view.

Below, the architrave of the Temple of Saturn resting on columns with Ionic capitals. The inscription recalls a fire that damaged the temple.

HOUSE OF THE VESTALS

This building, traditionally attributed to Numa Pompilio, was the home of the priestesses of Vesta. It was rebuilt by Nero following the fire of 64 AD and was later restructured many times. The adjacent buildings along the *Via Sacra* were in imperial times used as shops.

TEMPLE OF SATURN

Erected in 497 BC by Titus Tatius, the first dictator of Rome, on the site of the ancient altar dedicated to Saturn, the temple was restored many times before it was rebuilt in 42 BC by Lucius Munatius Plancus, one of Caesar's generals, with the booty from the Syrian campaign. The eight surviving columns date to the reconstruction of 283 AD.

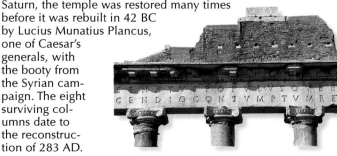

CIRCUS MAXIMUS

Although the Circus Maximus, the first construction of its kind in Rome, was initially built of wood, the sections in masonry gradually increased in number, beginning with the *carceres*, a sort of starting-gate for the horses. The circus consisted of a long track surrounded by a *cavea* with various tiers of seats, broken, on the side adjacent to the Palatine, by the *pulvinar*, a building with a tribune from which the emperor watched the contests.

The structure, which was modified repeatedly under Caesar, Augustus, Claudius, and Trajan, expanded to mammoth size until, under Constantine, it could contain more than 300,000 spectators. In 10 BC, Augustus installed an obelisk dedicated to the Sun, from Heliopolis in Egypt, on the *spina*, the central segment decorated with templets and statues around which the horses raced. This obelisk, today in Piazza del Popolo, was later flanked by another from the Temple of Ammon in Karnak, installed and dedicated to the Moon in about 357 AD by Constantius II and much later moved to Piazza San Giovanni in Laterano.

The last race in the Circus Maximus was run under Totila in 549; after this date it fell into ruin. It was used from the Middle Ages through modern times for the most disparate functions, until in the 1930s it was freed of the superstructures that had been added over time (to the exception of the Torre della Moletta) and the entire construction was again exposed.

A low relief showing the games and equestrian contests held in the Circus Maximus in honor of the god Consus, on the site of whose altar in the valley between the Palatine and the Aventine the circus was built. Legend attributes its foundation to Tarquinius Priscus (7th century BC).

View of the Circus Maximus.

THE OBELISK OF MONTECITORIO AND THE COLUMN OF MARCUS AURELIUS

Piazza Colonna. The Column of Marcus Aurelius, built in imitation of Trajan's Column.

The aspect to be given to Piazza di Montecitorio and Piazza Colonna was a centuries-old question that had often been debated and a final solution just as often put off. In the first case, the proposed solutions had been many; the last, advanced by Clement XI in the 18th century, called for re-erecting the Antonine Column, until that time preserved in the courtyard of the nearby Convento della Missione, at the center of a semicircular space. The plan was rejected; then, in 1792, Pio VI charged Giovanni Antinori with the task of setting up at the center of the square the **obelisk of Psammetychus II** - the gnomon of the *Horologium Augusti*. For its restoration, the architect made use of the porphyry of the Antonine Column; fittingly enough, with the addition of a perforated bronze globe, the gnomon, now column, again performed its original function and marked the hours on the paving stones of the square.

We might say that the circumstances leading to the creation of Piazza Colonna were instead entirely the opposite: the square was constructed, by order of Sixtus V, around the preexisting **Column of Marcus Aurelius**. On the model of Trajan's Column, it had originally been raised by the emperor on the ancient Via Flaminia, now Via del Corso, to commemorate the two campaigns against the Quadi, the Marcomanni, and the Sarmatians, brought to victorious conclusions between 172 and 175 AD and described in the long frieze that spirals around the shaft. In 1589, the pope had the column detached from its original base and restored; a bronze statue of *Saint Paul* gazing in the direction of the Vatican was placed at its top.

Trajan's Column topped by the statue of Saint Peter, in the Imperial Forums.

TRAJAN'S COLUMN

Five years after the end of the last of the two campaigns conducted between 101 and 108 AD by the emperor Trajan against the Dacians, an ancient Danubian population that occupied the territory that is today Rumania, the senate and the Roman people voted to celebrate Trajan's achievements with the erection of a column, probably designed by Apollodorus of Damascus, the architect who had planned the other buildings of Trajan's Forum. The column was raised at the center of the quadrangular courtyard on which opened the two libraries, Latin and Greek, facing each other on the short sides, and, on the long sides, the Temple of the Divus Trajanus and the Basilica Ulpia.

Set on a base decorated with reliefs depicting the Dacian weapons taken as trophies, the barrel of the *centenaria* column (called thus due to its height: 100 Roman feet or about 40 meters), is entirely covered with a spiral relief, 200 meters in length and containing more than 2500 figures, that describes the emperor's exploits. Trajan's ashes were preserved in a golden urn interred in the base of the column. The column was topped by a bronze statue of Trajan that was lost in the Middle Ages and replaced by the *Saint Peter* installed by Sixtus V in 1587.

The height of Trajan's column, as we are reminded by an inscription on the base, reflects the height of the spur of the Quirinal hill that was excavated to make room for the buildings of Trajan's colossal Forum.

The Ara Pacis Augustae. A general view of the enclosure; bottom, a detail of the frieze of the Procession.

An aerial view of the Ara Pacis and the Mausoleum of Augustus.

THE ARA PACIS AUGUSTAE AND THE MAUSOLEUM OF AUGUSTUS

Consecrated in 9 BC to celebrate the return of peace following the Gallic and Spanish campaigns, the altar was originally erected, by order of Augustus, on the Via Flaminia, today's Via del Corso, near the famous *Horologium Augusti* and what is now the site of the church of San Lorenzo in Lucina, in the *Campus Martius* area that at the time was dedicated to the glorification of the emperor. The altar was unearthed during archaeological excavations conducted in the late 1930s and moved to a pavilion built specially to house it. The Ara Pacis consists of a rectangular enclosure decorated on all four sides by a lower band of elegant decorations in the form of acanthus branches, and by a series of reliefs. Those to the sides of the entrance show the *Lupercale,* the grotto in which the she-wolf nursed Romulus and Remus, and the *Sacrifice of Aeneas to the Penates;* on the opposite side are found, in correspondence to the first two reliefs, *Peace* and the *Goddess*

Rome. In the relief of the *Procession for the Consecration of the Altar* that runs along the short sides, the figures of the emperor Augustus and his family are clearly identifiable. Inside the enclosure, which is decorated on the inner face with bucrania and garlands, is the altar as such; it was originally adorned with female figures and scenes of the annual sacrifice. Facing the Ara Pacis is the **Mausoleum of Augustus**, ordered built by the emperor as the tomb of the Julian-Claudian dynasty in 27 BC, the year in which he was proclaimed *Augustus* by the Roman senate following the successful Egyptian campaign. Originally, this was a structure consisting of concentric circular tiers planted with cypress trees, at the center of which rose a colossal column topped by a gilded bronze statue of the emperor. A cell in the column held Augustus' ashes, while his family members were buried in the ring immediately surrounding it. The entrance to the mausoleum was flanked by two **obelisks**, which today stand one on the Esquiline in front of Santa Maria Maggiore and the other on the fountain in Piazza del Quirinale.

103

Castel Sant'Angelo. An aerial view of the fortress and a part of the walls.

Left, the Mausoleum of Hadrian and a detail of fragments of entablatures.

Below, the bronze statue of the Archangel Michael placed on the summit of Castel Sant'Angelo in the 1700s.

CASTEL SANT'ANGELO

The massive fort that reflects in the waters of the Tiber, known as Castel Sant'Angelo, was originally the **Mausoleum of Hadrian**, designed and built by the emperor in 130 AD as his final resting place and the tomb of the members of the Antonine dynasty. The building consisted of a quadrangular base with an entrance in the form of a triumphal arch, which gave access, through a long corridor and a spacious vestibule (both still visible), to the overlying structures; the whole was topped by a gilded bronze sculptural group of a quadriga driven by the emperor. The overall effect was that of a gigantic Etruscan-style tumulus tomb, on the model of the Mausoleum of Augustus. The burial chamber at the center, in which were preserved the urns containing the ashes of Hadrian and his family members (and which later sheltered those of his successors through Caracalla), was accessed through a **helicoidal gallery** that despite later drastic remodeling is still recognizable.

Under Aurelian, the mausoleum became part of the defensive system raised to protect the *Pons Aelius*, today's **Ponte Sant'Angelo**, while still continuing to play its original role as a place of burial. In the meantime some of its original structures had been dismantled and reused in the construction of new buildings. This was the fate of the Parian marble rustication that sheathed the exterior, the colossal bronze peacocks, now in the Cortile del Belvedere in the Vatican, and the marble columns of the imperial sacellum, used to decorate the Basilica di San Paolo.

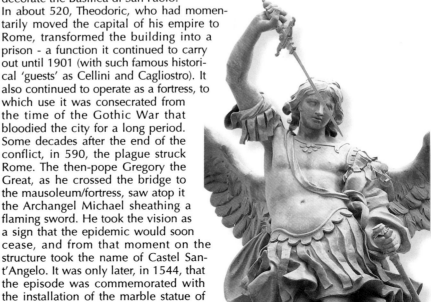

In about 520, Theodoric, who had momentarily moved the capital of his empire to Rome, transformed the building into a prison - a function it continued to carry out until 1901 (with such famous historical 'guests' as Cellini and Cagliostro). It also continued to operate as a fortress, to which use it was consecrated from the time of the Gothic War that bloodied the city for a long period. Some decades after the end of the conflict, in 590, the plague struck Rome. The then-pope Gregory the Great, as he crossed the bridge to the mausoleum/fortress, saw atop it the Archangel Michael sheathing a flaming sword. He took the vision as a sign that the epidemic would soon cease, and from that moment on the structure took the name of Castel Sant'Angelo. It was only later, in 1544, that the episode was commemorated with the installation of the marble statue of

Castel Sant'Angelo. An image of the walls and two spaces within the fortress.

Below, view of Castel Sant'Angelo from the bridge with the statues, designed by Bernini, alluding to the Passion of Christ.

the *Archangel Michael* by Raffaello da Montelupo in the place the apparition had been seen. The original angel was replaced, in 1752, by the bronze copy by Verschaffelt.

During the Middle Ages, the fortress became especially important for defense of the Vatican. In the ninth century, Pope Leo IV made it an integral part of that system of walls that delimited the area known as the 'Leonine City' and by which it was linked to many other buildings, including the nearby Vatican Palace. In the 13th century, under Pope Nicholas III, an overhead corridor was added along this stretch of the walls. Known as the **Passetto** or the **Borgo Corridor**, the passageway was restructured and perfected in the following centuries to permit the popes to reach Castel Sant'Angelo quickly in case of danger. The first pope of the modern age, Alexander VI, had Giuliano da Sangallo reinforce the castle with construction of a four-sided surrounding **wall** with four octagonal corner **towers** named for the four evangelists, a series of new bastions, and a wide moat. A few years later,

under Julius II, the marble **loggia** overlooking the Tiber was added; Paul III, fearing a Turkish invasion of the coasts of Latium, commissioned Antonio Sangallo the Younger to completely renovate the defensive installations and to enlarge the papal apartments in the castle. The rooms were decorated by Perin del Vaga and his studio in the mid-16th century with cycles of frescoes inspired by the *History of the Church* (**Sala Paolina**), and with figures from classical mythology (**Camera del Perseo**, **Camera di Amore and Psyche**).

But for the most part, the aspect of Castel Sant'Angelo is still that of a fortress built for defense, with its armed bastions complete with batteries of cannon, the **Armory** of Clement X built by Bernini and later transformed into the Chapel of the Condannati (prisoners awaiting execution in the **Courtyard of the Angel**), the so-called **Oliare**, large rooms and silos used to store foodstuffs for use in case of siege, and the parapet walk, which still today offers the visitor a full view of the Vatican and indeed of much of Rome.

PALAZZO SENATORIO

This building stands on a site on which functions linked to the political life of the city have always been carried on. It was originally that of the **Tabularium**, housing the state archives, ordered built by Quintus Lutatius Catulus in 78 BC. In the eighth century, the senate of Rome met in the Curia, but when this old building was damaged and isolated by the marshes that were invading the forum, it was decided to reorganize administrative activity in another location. The first site chosen was the cloister, today no longer in existence, of Santa Maria in Aracoeli, but later, as city independence grew and with it the prestige of the senators, a more fitting meeting-place was sought. Thus, in 1143, work began for construction of a new building on the ruins of the *Tabularium*. It was remodeled in 1299, when a loggia and two corner towers were also added. The building was severely damaged by the troops of Holy Roman emperor Henry VII but was restored in the early 15th century under Pope Boniface IX, who donated it to the city of Rome. Pope Nicholas V had the central tower added, but the building took on its modern-day look only a century later, under Pope Paul III, who charged Michelangelo with redesigning it.

Michelangelo in person directed the work of building the **staircase**; it was later decorated by order of Sixtus V with the statue of the goddess *Roma Capitolina*, originally Minerva, in the center niche, and those of the *Nile* and the *Tiber* (originally the *Tigris*), brought to the Capitoline from the Baths of Constantine on the Quirinal hill, in those on each side. The work planned by Michelangelo was completed, with some liberties taken, between 1582 and 1605 by Giacomo Della Porta, Girolamo Rainaldi, and Martino Longhi the Elder, who is also the author of the brick **bell tower** that replaced the medieval turret.

Palazzo Senatorio. The porphyry-and-marble statue of Roma Capitolina.

Piazza del Campidoglio. A view toward the city; at the center of the square, the copy of the equestrian statue of Marcus Aurelius that has replaced the restored original, now in the Capitoline Museums.

Palazzo Senatorio, seat of Rome city government, at the top of the cordonata, *with on the left Palazzo Nuovo and on the right Palazzo dei Conservatori.*

Piazza Navona. The facade of the church of Sant'Agnese in Agone and that of the adjacent Palazzo Pamphili; in the foreground, the Fontana del Moro.

PIAZZA NAVONA

If this square is one of the most famous in the world, it is justly so thanks to the sumptuous monuments facing on it and the fountains that decorate its center. The square has in fact always been a space for games and spectacles, and it was so even before Domitian chose the site for his **Stadium**, inaugurated with the *Agoni Capitolini* in 86 AD. Even after its decline began in the 5th century, the arena continued to be the site of games, jousts, festivals, and spectacles of every type; beginning in 1477 it was also the home of the city market, transferred here from the Campidoglio. The role played by the site throughout history also determined its name. 'Navona' is a corruption of the Latin expression *in agone,* used to describe the square in the Middle Ages.

And while it preserved the form and the dimensions of the ancient Stadium, the square meanwhile began to acquire its characteristic look. In the 13th century its perimeter was constellated by a long line of tower-homes belonging to the most important Roman families; during the Quattrocento they were replaced by sumptuous patrician residences like **Palazzo Orsini** and **Palazzo De Cupis**, and by the church of San Giacomo degli Spagnoli, today known as **Nostra Signora del Sacro Cuore**. The square was paved during the papacy of Innocent VIII, and in the 16th century Gregory XIII installed the **Fontana del Moro** and the **Fontana del Nettuno**, both by Giacomo Della Porta. The fountains take their names from the statues that currently adorn the basins: respectively, the *Moor Fighting a Dolphin*, a 17th-century

work by Antonio Mari, and the 19th-century *Neptune Fighting an Octopus*. In the early 17th century new building were added, such as **Palazzo Millini** and **Palazzo Pamphili**. It was a member of the latter family, Giovanni Battista (who became Pope Innocent X in 1644), who gave Piazza Navona its present aspect, employing the talents of the most celebrated architects of the age: Bernini, Borromini, Pietro da Cortona, and Girolamo and Carlo Rainaldi. The latter was commissioned to build the church of **Sant'Agnese in Agone**, which was, however, completed by Borromini. And of the same architect the pope initially commissioned the **Fontana dei Quattro Fiumi** (Fountain of the Four Rivers) as an ornament for the center of the square, but in the end gave the nod to Bernini's more fanciful and theatrical sketch of a rock rising at the center of the pool, surmounted by an obelisk with the allegorical representations of the four greatest rivers on Earth as symbols of the four known continents (Asia, Europe, America, and Africa): the *Ganges*, by Purissimi; the *Danube*, by Raggi; the *Rio de la Plata* by Baratta; and the *Nile*, portrayed by Fancelli with her face covered because at the time the sources were yet unknown.

The legend that grew up around the rivalry between the two greatest Baroque architects recounts that the *Nile* is shown blindfolded as not to have to observe Borromini's facade of Sant'Agnese, and that the extended arm of the statue of the *Rio de la Plata* alludes to its imminent collapse. The legend, of course, has no historical foundation whatsoever, since Bernini completed the fountain in 1651, a year before work began for the construction of the church.

FONTANA DI TREVI

The legend runs that a nymph led the exhausted troops of the consul Marcus Vispanius Agrippa to drink at a spring, which in honor of the divine maiden was named Vergine; a while later, in 19 BC, Agrippa directed its waters into a distribution system that he called Acqua Vergine, after the same nymph. Damaged by neglect and time, the aqueduct was restored in the mid-15th century under Pope Nicholas V, who ordered that there be built a fountain supplied by its waters near that *trivium* that lent its name to whole Trevi district.

About three centuries later, in 1732 to be exact, Pope Clement XII decided to replace the original fount with a grander, more majestic construction. The architect Nicola Salvi, taking his inspiration from drawings by Bernini, gave form to a sort of monumental theatrical backdrop against one of the sides of Palazzo Poli, a marvelous union of architecture and sculpture.

The focal point of Salvi's invention is Pietro Bracci's statue of *Oceanus* standing on a shell-shaped chariot pulled by seahorses led by tritons, the work of Maini. The stately sculptural group moves on a rocky podium enlivened by plants and fabulous creatures of all kinds. In the side niches there instead stand two allegorical statues, by Filippo Valle, of *Salubrity* and *Abundance*; these are surmounted by two low reliefs of the *Virgin Nymph Leading Agrippa's Troops to the Spring* and *Agrippa Ordering Construction of the Aqueduct*, by Bergondi and Grossi, respectively. Topping the structure, supported by Corinthian columns, is an elaborate attic with a dedicatory inscription, the statues of the *Four Seasons*, and, on the balustrade at the summit, the *coat-of-arms of Pope Clement XII* between the two allegorical figures of *Fame*. The complex structure of the fountain was thirty years in the building, and was completed only under Pope Clement XIII.

The Fontana di Trevi against the triumphal arch crowned by the coat-of-arms of Pope Clement XII.

PIAZZA DEL POPOLO

The present layout of the square is the 19th-century work of Giuseppe Valadier, whose intent it was to integrate architecture and landscape. He exploited the natural slope of the Pincio and remodeled the earlier trapezoidal form of the square, at the center of which rose the **Flaminian Obelisk**, an Egyptian granite monolith from the time of Rameses II, brought here from the Circus Maximus where it had been placed by Augustus. The two hemicycles of the square were decorated with fountains with allegorical statues: *Neptune and Two Tritons* toward the Tiber, and the *Goddess Rome between the Tiber and the Aniene Rivers* on the side toward the Pincio.

THE PANTHEON

The Pantheon is, naturally, one of the symbols of Rome, but it is also and above all one of the points of reference for the architecture of all times, a constant source of inspiration and a model that has been imitated countless times over the centuries. Conceived as an *Augusteum*, or sacred site dedicated to the deified emperor Augustus, and then, as the name implies, as the *Temple of All the Gods* protectors of his family, it was built in 27 BC by Augustus' son-in-law Marcus Vispanius Agrippa. Agrippa's statue, together with that of his powerful relative, originally occupied one of the two niches at the sides of the entrance portal. The building was damaged during the fire of 80 AD and was restored by Domitian and by Trajan; it was later totally rebuilt in 118-125 by Hadrian, to whom the plans of the present building are attributed.

The temple thus changed form and orientation, from a simple four-sided structure to a complex construction defined by the association of a cylindrical body surmounted by a hemispherical dome of equal diameter and height and preceded by a rectangular **pronaos**. The pronaos is in turn measured by 16 monolithic columns in grey and pink granite, topped with Corinthian marble capitals; it is crowned by a pediment with a **tympanum**, which was originally decorated with a bronze frieze. Bronze also sheathed the ceiling of the pronaos, but it was ordered removed in 1625 by Pope Urban VIII Barberini for use by Bernini for the Baldacchino of Saint Peter's and for casting the cannons of Castel Sant'Angelo. The populace commented this act with the famous pasquinade: *Quod non fecerunt barbari fecerunt Barberini* ("What the barbarians didn't do, the Barberinis did").

The structure of the **rotunda**, which is linked to the pronaos by a rectangular brick structure faced in marble, reveals a complex cosmic symbolism in the *seven niches* in the drum, one for each of the planetary divinities (Venus, Mars, Jupiter, Saturn, Uranus, Neptune, and Pluto), and the five orders of *lacunars* in the interior of the dome; over it all there opens the *oculus*, symbol of the disk of the Sun and the only source of illumination for the building.

The **dome**, the largest ever created in masonry, is built of an especially light agglomerate of mortar and chips of travertine that are replaced higher up with gravel and pumice.

When it was donated in 608 by the emperor Phocas to Pope Boniface IV, the temple was transformed into the church of Santa Maria dei Martiri, and despite the transformations it underwent over the course of the centuries the structure remained virtually unaltered down through our times. After 1870, when the two small bell towers at the sides (the so-called 'donkeys' ears' commissioned of Bernini by Urban VIII) were demolished, the Pantheon was transformed into the memorial chapel of the kings of Italy, whose tombs began to flank the previously-installed *Tomb of Raphael*, decorated with the famous *Madonna del Sasso* painted by Lorenzetto in 1520 on commission from Raphael himself.

Top, the Flaminian Obelisk at the center of Piazza del Popolo.

The Pantheon. Above, a view of the interior; left, the pronaos.